How to be
HEADHUNTED

How to be

HEADHUNTED

HOW TO MAKE YOURSELF THE BEST PERSON FOR THE BEST JOB

Yvonne Sarch

C

CENTURY
BUSINESS

First published in the UK in 1991 by Business Books Limited
First published in paperback in 1992 by Century Business
An imprint of Random Century Group Ltd
20 Vauxhall Bridge Road, London SW1V 2SA

Random Century Group Australia (Pty) Ltd
20 Alfred Street, Milsons Point
Sydney, NSW 2061, Australia

Random Century Group New Zealand Ltd
18 Poland Road, Glenfield
Auckland 10, New Zealand

Random Century Group South Africa (Pty) Ltd
PO Box 337, Bergvlei, South Africa

Printed and bound in Great Britain by
Mackays of Chatham PLC, Chatham, Kent

A catalogue record for this book is available
from the British Library.

ISBN 0–7126–9895–7

Contents

CONTENTS

Introduction

'I saw the angel in the marble and I just chiselled 'till I set him free.'
Michelangelo.

What did you see in the mirror this morning?

The image that greeted you is the one that the outside world views. It is the face that expresses your personality, ambitions and opinions. How you look and behave communicate essential things about you to your staff, colleagues and superiors. But do you *really* know whether these visual and behavioural signposts convey the correct information? Are they saying what you want them to say or are there facets of your personality – skills, abilities, ideas and opinions – which remain locked up and hidden from the outside world? What goes on in your head may, however, be entirely different, and it is this which must be explored and developed so that the visible image can be managed and enriched accordingly.

Do you seek feedback from family, friends, colleagues, bosses and anyone else who is in a position to have an opinion about you? Perhaps they give it unsolicited – the point is, do you listen? Do you know how to decipher which aspects of your public image need checking, or even changing?

However misguided or apparently unjustified, the opinions of others are a useful tool in developing your self-awareness. This early awareness of your reputation – of how others see you – can help you to identify choices and decide on the steps which will lead you towards your ultimate goal. This goal will be more easily realized if it can be communicated and visualized – rather than simply idealized in your head.

Today you are probably earning enough to be independent and mobile, own a home, and have a job which is stretching your abilities. But if you want to maintain this, and progress even further, you need to study who you are and where you are heading next.

In particular you need to decide if you want to reach the top of your profession – if you do you must commit your time and energy to ensuring that everyone around you recognizes where you are aiming to go. Managing your own professional reputation will open new doors and bring new contacts. As Peter Breen, of Heidrich & Struggles, says: 'To be headhunted you must have a reputation for being one of the best. Then the top firms will find you'. Kit Power of Spencer Stuart also asserts: 'You must be known, you must be known to be very good and you must be known for what you are very good at'. However, as Julia Budd of Egon Zender explains: 'Profile management is no real substitute for real achievement'.

This book is to help you in your personal search to be 'one of the best'. It will show you how to become 'visible' and remain so, by learning to:

- Know the environment you are working in – your company, sector, industry – and to know what is going on in the market
- Understand yourself better and define what you want from your personal and professional life – only then can you formulate your long-term career goals and take responsibility for your professional development
- Develop yourself and your reputation by learning from bosses and mentors, taking advantage of training opportunities and being a more effective leader
- Survive the stresses and strains of your responsibilities at work

and at home and maintain your reputation
- Reach for the top by taking risks and being visible – knowing how to build on your reputation

You are Michelangelo's 'angel in the marble'. Now is the time to start chiselling, to reveal your full beauty, character, and capabilities.

Part I

· 1 ·

The Beginnings of Your Reputation

How do you get headhunted?

After some serious reflection, you have decided that you want to excel in your profession: what should be your first steps to achieve what may well seem a daunting goal? How do you begin to manage your career and reputation in practical and manageable bite sizes?

The most important step is to recognize that your professional performance and reputation are indivisible – they are two sides of the coin. Forgetting this, or allowing yourself to concentrate on one at the expense of the other, will lead only to trouble. A professional reputation which cannot be substantiated by real success is something that people will eventually see through and perhaps despise you for. Similarly, high quality performance which is recognized and acknowledged by a few people only will mean that you never achieve the success, rewards and status that you really deserve.

Managing these two aspects of your career simultaneously can ensure that nothing you do or achieve is wasted. It ensures that your professional reputation always reflects solid business performance. After all, there is often nothing more impressive than meeting someone with a prestigious reputation and discovering that they truly deserve this – a rare event in today's work environment and because of this perhaps all the more memorable!

The next step towards managing your reputation and career is to reach a deeper sense of self-awareness and objectivity. You need to understand how your achievements and behaviour at work are shaped by your inner needs and drives. How do these drives affect your everyday attitudes and behaviour? Which should you cultivate and which should you try to change?

To aid you in this process of self-recognition, this chapter explores how family experiences mould your personality and affect some of your deepest attitudes towards such things as success, power and achievement. The chapter goes on to examine personal motivation – the needs and goals that drive you on in your career – and looks at what some of the major motivational theorists have to say. Understanding these personal and professional factors will give you vital clues about how to maximize your own and other people's motivation.

Hand in hand with motivation is what you actually achieve – your attention and commitment to quality performance. If you want to reach the top, or to get to where you want to go, you need to make quality performance both a consuming passion and a competitive weapon. And all of this will, of course, demand boundless energy and stamina. If you are not to be defeated from realizing your full potential, you need to manage your lifestyle in a way that keeps you in top form.

Finally, it helps to place all these issues – early formative experiences, motivation, attention to quality, and energy and stamina – into the larger context of career life cycles. Whether you are in your twenties or sixties, you need to understand the life stage through which you are travelling. Only by doing so will you be able to capitalize on your experiences to the full and yet be ready to move into the next career life cycle.

1.1 FAMILY INFLUENCE

Parents see their children as belonging to them. Families are the systems in which the whole is greater than the parts: as an individual within the family you can be trapped into roles and rituals which are well-practised and full of rules.

In the family system, each person plays a part. Without the interaction between parents, children and close relatives, there is no system. This is where you have learnt to cohabit and coexist with others – and you may carry the level of success or failure achieved there into your adult and working life.

Your position in the family can often give you certain advantages and disadvantages. The following descriptions of family roles are crude generalizations. You may find them very helpful to see where you are situated and to think about taking remedial action from that point.

If you are a *first* child you will tend to make decisions and hold values consistent with, or in exact opposition to, your father. You will tend to be socially aware, conscious of the needs of others and sensitive to social norms and images. You will thrive on things and ideas which are explicit and obvious. You will look for detail and be ruled by your head rather than your heart. You may have some difficulty developing self-esteem because you have had to justify yourself against overt control from new, nervous parents.

If you are a *second* child, you are likely to be more emotionally orientated and to react instinctively to family needs and unwritten family rules. You are likely to bond more closely with your mother. You may be the clown of the family, using your humour and talent to lighten tension and distract others from conflict. You may act out the unconscious needs and desires of your mother and become an extension of her life. If you are male, you may fulfil the fantasy of the man she never married; if you are female, your mother may try to enable you to do the things she always wanted to do. Perhaps you have trouble connecting your head and your heart as both are governed by your intuition. You can appear naive and puzzled while in fact you are picking up the hidden agendas within the family system.

As a *third* child, you may try to look into the relationship needs of the system and tend to identify with the marriage relationship. You may have a hard time finding your own individuality because of the strength of the influence of the parental bond and how your father and mother relate to each other. You may feel very ambivalent and have trouble making choices, appearing to be uninvolved while in fact being very involved.

As a *fourth* child, you will be in the unfortunate position of catching and collecting unresolved family tensions. You will pick up signals and become part of the interactions, yet feel powerless to do anything about what is going on. You may try to be the cute, sweet family mascot to try and distract from your position in the family. You can appear both infantile and indulged, as well as disruptive and outrageous to other members of the family.

Further children tend to repeat the fourth child's behaviour, taking over his or her position as the youngest. *Only* children emulate the parent they believe to be the stronger.

Within the family group, the role of the parent is to be a model man or woman, showing how to be an adult and how to express feelings and desires. The role of children is to be curious and learn. In functioning families the roles are flexible, but in dysfunctioning families the roles become rigid.

The need to be unique and self-aware often clashes with the need to conform for the sake of the system. However being aware of standards, and being unwilling to drop them whatever the pressure, is part of gaining a reputation. It is easier to follow this code if you have had positive parental role models. High standards show in consistent quality of performance and good judgment. This consistency adds up to being known for your integrity.

Most of us will find our behaviour as adults shaped to some degree by our early experiences. For example, you have not had great praise as a child, in fact if you have had to justify your existence from an early age, you will be looking for recognition for the rest of your life. It will be vital to you to have employment with a blue-chip company within which you can make your mark. This is a better way of justifying your existence – by achievement – rather than by excusing yourself and feeling a failure.

Those of you who want achievement and recognition, whatever your status, can never have enough and will continue to look for more. Yet fame and fortune are the goals of the few, found by the few and held only for a while. Andy Warhol said that everyone can be famous for fifteen minutes – *you* are aiming for a professional reputation which lasts longer.

In order to begin building this reputation, you should not be afraid of receiving and appreciating praise. Traditionally the British are not very good at taking compliments and react with suspicion when praised aloud. Many individuals are the same. Yet think how much better you work when someone has noticed what you have done – and said so. The value of praise increases when it is from 'above', or said in public. Most of us need to court recognition from those senior to us to increase our self-esteem so that we can perform better. Of course, there is always the unscrupulous boss who will use praise to motivate without backing it up with promotion or other recognition, and you should learn to evaluate the person who is giving praise as well as the praise itself. Similarly, when you are the boss, you should ensure your praise is perceived as valuable – your encouragement will mean something to your staff only if you have earned their respect. Public recognition is not quite the same as private recognition. You may be praised for a 'one-off' action as much as for a continuous performance, for example, an actor may become an overnight success for playing a part in a major film after 20 long years have been spent treading the repertory boards.

Reputation is the culmination of recognition both private and public, and is long lasting. What people think of you may not always be based on totally accurate information, but your track record does matter.

1.2 PERSONAL MOTIVATION

The things which motivate you to perform a job include both personal and professional factors. Your needs, drives and goals are interlinked with the work itself and its rewards. As you come to understand what propels you forward you will also gain a richer insight into the most effective ways of motivating others. In this way, self-awareness can directly transfer into effective management and motivating skills.

It used to be considered necessary constantly to supervise people and work, because it was assumed that people are basically lazy and only motivated by rewards and money. Nowadays, the more usual assumption is that people are self-motivated, and that as self-starters they are looking for autonomy and are seeking more satisfaction from work than just the pay-cheque at the end of the month. Doubtless you will have discovered that your behaviour can be triggered by certain methods or approaches to your work, such as recognizing or setting meaningful targets. The process through which you go to achieve them, includes choices which will have to be made in order to achieve the goal. When you repeat the process you are reinforcing the ways which are most effective in reaching your objectives, rather than wasting time on less productive methods.

In order to deepen your own understanding about your own and others' motivation it is useful to discover what some of the leading motivational theorists had to say. When in 1954 Dr Abraham Maslow theorized on the motivation of the individual, for example, he postulated that personal needs are the primary focus and mechanism for human motivation and action. When your needs are satisfied your behaviour is influenced and your work becomes less challenging. Your basic needs have a hierarchy ranging from food and shelter to fulfilling your ego and achieving your goals. When your survival needs are satisfied, ie when you have a roof over your head and food to eat, you move on to wanting other things such as a car, more home comforts etc, and then on to successful accomplishment of tasks for their own sake. Thus Maslow's hierarchy of needs is:

a) Physiological
b) Safety and security
c) Social and belonging
d) Ego, status and self-esteem
e) Self-actualization

Each of these five levels of need can be applied to your workplace. You can use them when identifying what motivates you, your colleagues or your staff.

The two-factor theory put forward in 1959 by Frederick Herzberg followed Maslow and has been widely used in management thinking. He developed his ideas based on a survey of 200 accountants and engineers, from which he discovered that they were more satisfied with their work when they felt they were doing good work and accomplishing something which involved challenge. Do you identify with these findings? Do you feel dissatisfied when the rewards are meagre and the working conditions poor?

Currently, one of the most accepted and practised theories is Alderfer's ERG theory. Alderfer (in 1972) sought to establish 'human needs in organizational settings', and condensed Maslow's hierarchy into E (existence), R (relatedness) and G (growth): E covers A and B of Maslow's hierarchy; R overlaps B, C and D; G rounds off D and E.

What you expect from your work or workers will affect your style of management and increase or decrease motivation accordingly. When you understand that people have certain attitudes to work and place certain values on work-related rewards, then you can influence the effort-performance-reward relationships in planning strategy and in implementation.

When you compare your input into, or outcome of, your work with that of others, or when you compare the work of one individual with another, then you are trying to be fair in your assessment. When there is equity in these comparisons, the individuals involved will be satisfied – otherwise you will be dissatisfied or will be creating discontent. This happens most often when you are carrying out performance appraisal with a view to relating pay or rewards.

The use of your power to reward or punish, which you will recognize from your school-days, is one of your primary mechanisms of authority as a manager. When there is an organized system in the workplace for giving praise or criticism, or there is a good chance of promotion, based on managerial assessment, then there will be related motivation to perform well depending on how fair you are being seen to be in your judgement. This will be reflected down the line of reporting so that even the most junior member of staff will be motivated accordingly.

So, whether you are setting goals either for yourself or others, these mechanisms of motivation also come into play. In simple terms, easy goals increase performance; harder goals result in higher performance. You have to give direction to others and maximize motivation so that everyone can perform to the maximum of his or her potential.

At the end of the day there is no hard and fast rule for maximizing your own motivation or for motivating others – you need to analyse each situation as it arises and assess which of the particular techniques or methods you have developed will be the most useful in causing and sustaining the motivation you need in different work circumstances.

1.3 QUALITY OF PERFORMANCE

If you really want to get ahead, start a quality improvement focus in your work; it can become both a consuming passion and a competitive weapon. A good time to begin is when there is a change of circumstance, eg, a new boss or a new building.

As far as your clients are concerned, your objectives in fulfilling their needs and expectations must be identified, then met by performance through a careful detailed process. For example, in executive search, you should have candidate papers prepared and circulated in good time for the interviewing panel to be well briefed before the appointment panel date.

In further understanding what influences your performance the work of David McClelland at Harvard in the late 1906s still has a value in profiling how you as an individual function in relation to the nature of the job.

McClelland identifies the following three personality drives:

- *Achievement* – the need to do things well and, as much as possible, by one's self from beginning to end
- *Affiliation* – the need to maintain close inter-personal relationships, even if this means compromising the objective requirement of the tasks
- *Power* – the need to feel strong or to justify one's self by exercising influence or making an impact on others

McClelland goes on to sub-divide these personality types into a detailed set of needs and attitudes. They include the following: The need for *achievement* is defined as:

- Growth – Self-imposed standards, mastery of the difficult, willingness to change, desire to learn, use of experts, processing failure, personal or product improvement, unique accomplishment
- Endurance – Internal control, persevering effort, risk calculation, reliable follow through, overcoming of obstacles, concentration on technique, hardiness under stress

The need for *affiliation* is defined as:

- Relations – maintaining friendly contacts, involvement in long-term relationships, insisting on inclusion, exchanging personal anecdotes, manoeuvering to be accepted, concern for popularity, commiseration with others
- Nurturance – capacity for empathy, compassion for sympathetic persons, ministering consolation, comfort, or service to others, sensitivity to body language, non-threatening communication, coaching skill, supportive relationships
- Deference – self-abasement, resignation, ingratiation of authority, conformance to peer pressure, passive, deflecting, avoiding, smoothing, or compromising conflict management style

The need for *power* is defined as:

- Dominance – assuming leadership, commanding others, insisting on discipline, exercising control, shaping others, negotiating/persuading, forceful or opinionated actions
- Exhibition – image projection, impression management, behavioural rehearsal and role play, clever or witty statements, exuberant/intemperant social behaviour, monitoring of audience response
- Recognition – concern for reputation or professional prestige, desirous of credit, striving for status position, decision-making authority or winning awards, maintenance of visible or instrumental associations

The breakdown of these three characteristics into needs and

attitudes is very useful in working out your own managerial profile.

Never assume that your current level of performance and production is as excellent as possible. You should be identifiable by the quality of your work and *differentiated* by the high calibre of your performance. There will always be emergencies, mistakes, oversights, but by thinking 'quality' you can increase the level of excellence from this moment.

Good client relations start with the original presentation, then proposal, then performance. A reputation for quality, customer care and delivery is essential for continuous success in winning the business, completing and following on. Your company, group or cost centre will be more profitable, busy, and successful when the aim is to be 'the best'. For example, in most companies, bonuses for individuals depend on the profitability of their team. By interacting to meet the target, bonuses too improve.

Hamish Kidd of Clive & Stokes International believes in promoting a high quality, efficient and personal service based on the company's aim to be flexible and responsive to client's needs. Then we all benefit from repeat business and earn our bonuses regularly.

Your quality improvement focus can be broken down into the following aides-memoires:

- Better-than-most/best service – gains and keeps clients
- Doing it right first time increases your turnover and therefore affects your bonus
- The firm that works for quality (excellence) thrives
- You are not indispensable – there is always another person who can do your job. Can they do it as well? Your insurance policy for progress and security is to be better, better, better
- Announce any change which will be effective/efficient and incorporate it into the system

How good you are will be indicated by:

- Increased business and profits
- Having new clients

- Commitment from the top cascading down the line to all levels
- Having controls to prevent errors escalating
- having clarity of targets, rationale of method and knowledge of achievement
- A management culture which gives feedback and encouragement to all, and praise when due
- Recognition of success, whether at individual or corporate level
- The use of cross-functioning (co-ordinating efforts and skills) for corporate gain
- Ensuring that the group/division/team when individually successful, is also matching corporate goals

Quality in work increases motivation and energy for you – and leads to success for all.

Are the rules for building up a professional reputation the same for men and women? The successful advancement of women into management during the last decade shows that women have been learning to play the corporate game very successfully. By following the development pattern of career men, they have and will continue to succeed. However, total success will not be gained through being 'chaps in skirts' – women will win by being themselves.

Those men and women competing for top executive jobs know they have to play by the rules, accept the corporate culture and add to their competence with wide experience. In some cases these rules will penalize women with family responsibilities. Unfortunately, the need for special understanding of family commitments, and for provision of certain facilities for working women is something yet to be realized by many companies. This may change with the shifting demographics, which should encourage employers to be more hospitable to women. However, the progress, so far, of corporate women has met considerable resistance and is much slower than it should be. The next generation of senior women, at present in their early stages of acquiring qualifications and training, will be more familiar to their male peers and will be greatly needed in the labour market. If you fall into this category you may (justifiably) live in hope.

1.4 DETERMINATION

Once you see yourself in a situation, job or whatever, you are halfway to doing it – and doing it well. Often when I have briefed candidates and matched their experience to the criteria of the appointment, I can detect whether or not they will be selected by their ability to visualize themselves in the future. Some are convinced easily; others may want the job but cannot really see themselves in the position. Some candidates can visualize themselves doing the job, regardless of their track record, and it is these candidates who often stand the best chance of succeeding. A way to help heighten your awareness is by this four-step method:

1. Think of an idea.
2. Fantasize about making it happen.
3. Talk about it.
4. Do it.

However, living in the present, with your level of awareness fine-tuned, means that you will spot details which others may overlook. You will increase your abilities to analyse and act positively by cultivating concentration. The more you concentrate, the more you are absorbed in what you are doing, and the more you live in the present. The past creates experience and the future lies as yet untouched, but what you do in the present is the key to your destiny.

By being diligent, you will become less likely to be negligent: carelessness is avoidance of detail or lack of concentration. Instead of worrying, reduce your anxiety by taking considered action. Practice does help – and a problem will only remain a problem while you regard it as one. The stronger you are in your mind, the less problems will disturb you – this is the route to peace and contentment.

You have the wherewithal to achieve. The British notion of being unconquerable rose to the fore in wartime – the same notion can be applied on a personal level.

'Make extraordinary demands on yourself. Organizations are managed by example. In every structure there is one element which has to bear the load.' Peter Drucker.

As an afficionado of the management by walking around style, consider working outside your existing work space too. By actively participating in external company links you will bring enlightened understanding back to your team. You can fill in for absent members of your senior staff from time to time and discover what is expected from them by clients, what difficulties they have with deliveries, what interaction has been established in the market-place.

If you are disturbed by the influx of technology, and the use of information technology in particular, find out what information you need to make your leadership effective. Learn enough to be able to prioritize the data you need, and the systems which are essential.

Review the tasks you undertake as a matter of habit, and those which are recent and have been brought about by current needs, then decide to reduce the old and increase the new. This should be done as a rolling programme so that you are constantly up to date.

'What if' and other hypothetical possibilities add to your workload and block your thinking capacity. Find a method which incorporates contingency plans but keeps you in the present reality, with an eye on long-term planning but not multiple-possibility workloads.

Keep strong, healthy, active and up-to-date.

1.5 ENERGY AND STAMINA

Fatigue only becomes chronic if you do not re-stock your energy and deal with the daily weariness. Being tired is just part of life, but if rest and change does not make you feel better – then get yourself checked.

Some people have more energy than others. You should already have some idea of how much energy you are willing to expend on furthering your career and reputation. Generally speaking you have a choice as to how you spend your time and efforts, so the earlier you make a decision on your priorities, both in work and elsewhere, the better you will use your energy. This should be related to your abilities, goals, ambitions and rewards sought. It has little to do with the hours spent working, a great deal to do with the *use* of that time.

You can determine your energy level by considering your active hours versus sleeping hours and whether you participate in sports and other physical interests as well as work.

There is a difference between being a hyperactive workaholic and being energetic. Achieving a successful balancing act is when you enjoy being inactive in front of the television, playing bridge or reading a novel as well as scheming for the next order or winning another tennis match. Nothing is a waste of time – you never know how what you are doing will come in useful, or when the person you meet will become a client. By cultivating your whole person you will also add to your persona and create your own energy.

Stamina is what people envy if they have not found its secret themselves. It is the key to success. It is not simply a case of having a healthy body: it is one thing to have bags of energy, quite another to have staying power. Business is relentless, clients and production do not wait. You have to keep yourself in top form to meet challenges which usually arise just when you are least expecting them and are longing to put your feet up. Stamina is the ability to be always alert, ready to grasp an opportunity on the one hand and to withstand the trauma of disasters and upheavals on the other. Survival depends on stamina.

You need your career to establish who and what you are. You need energy to sustain your position and stamina to continue upwards.

Energy can run out. Some potential high-flyers plateau in their thirties, some fade out at a certain managerial level and others are content to remain where they have become familiar with the role. Energy means effort – an extra mile when you are tired, another file dealt with, another phone call made. Whatever the cause, the effect of low energy levels is to stunt careers, so it is imperative for you to learn to store energy.

'Personal fatigue is an indicator of how well we are faring in achieving our goals. Fatigue is an excellent gauge of well-being because it is a very hard symptom to mask,' says Dr Holly Atkinson author of *Women and Fatigue*. When you are tired, you are held back from performing at your best. By checking on the causes, and looking at possible corrections, you will feel better and so work better too.

When you have a medically diagnosed condition, you have to depend on your doctor for help; otherwise you will find yourself your own best physician. However, if you can identify chronic fatigue as a sympton, do persevere for medical evaluation so that disease can be ruled out. When checking yourself, start with noting just how often you feel tired and see if a pattern emerges. This may be linked to poor time management where you are not spreading your load well, or pressure from home. You will soon discover the habits and responsibilities that are wearing you out. Contributing habits are:

- Smoking – at any time
- Excessive alcohol consumption
- Sitting down for too many hours in the day
- Using chemicals, eg sleeping tablets
- Excessive dieting

Another factor leading to energy depletion is role conflict. For women, balancing domestic and professional responsibilities can be difficult. Men too have role confusion within the work hierarchy and in family leadership. The sheer physical daily grind falls more frequently to women, but men maintain that the pressure of earning the income necessary to keep the family is an equally constant pressure.

Options and choices do exist, even if you cannot see such miraculous solutions at first. Fighting fatigue may sound like the last thing you want to do – because you may use up your last bit of energy in the effort, but it is simply not acceptable to be constantly weary when you are in meetings, talking to clients and so on. In fact, the effort necessary to disguise that you are exhausted, for example when interviewing, takes up energy too and will probably leave you further exhausted at the end of the session.

An energy imbalance means that you are unable to deal effectively with complex problems and easily become irritable or unreasonable over trivial occurrencs. This leads to less and less effort being applied to the work in hand, shortcuts being taken and a significant drop in performance. This makes you appear inferior – which you are, in relation to your energetic colleagues.

Lethargy can manifest itself in different ways in different people: at one extreme is nausea, headache, dizziness and tremulousness, at the other is euphoria. It is not enough just to take an aspirin and try to carry on. You must stop and work out how often you are suffering and analyse what seems to trigger your weariness.

As with any profitable investment, your energy 'out' should be balanced with energy 'in.' Good food, exercise and undisturbed sleep, for example, are 'in'; poor nutrition, smoking and excessive alcohol consumption are 'out.'

IN	OUT
Good food	Poor nutrition
Plenty of exercise	Smoking
Undisturbed sleep	Too much alcohol
Fun	Illness
Control of your life	Stress at home/work
At least two weeks	Limited control
holiday p.a	of your life

When a situation, or perhaps proximity to a particular person occurs, adrenalin rises and energy is created. You should set up circumstances and meet people who have this effect, whenever possible. The balance of boosting and drawing of energy to make sure your well-being is being manufactured is worth considering.

You may find it easier than you think to change your lifestyle to meet the criteria. The popularity of designer mineral waters, for instance, accelerated the acceptance of drinking non-alcoholic drinks in company, at business lunches, etc. Smoking has also undergone social changes. In most workplaces, and often in restaurants and many modes of transport, smoking can only take place in designated areas.

By recognizing that you are weary, under par and not looking forward to another day's work, you are on the right track to correcting the problem. Like every other task you undertake, you may need to acquire some new skills to combat the symptoms. It is not spoiling yourself to have at least one and a half hours per 24 hours to yourself apart from sleeping. Even if you have to lock yourself in the bathroom and become deaf to demands in order to achieve this, it is *necessary*. The Americans describe this as 'taking time out', realizing that the 'payoff' is worthwhile. They also know that 'I'm just taking a nap' is another valuable aid.

1.6 THE BUSINESS LIFE-CYCLE

After family upbringing, school and college, you are launched into the world of work. Events after this time can pass with bewildering rapidity. However, if you are to appreciate and understand what is happening to you, you should recognize that there are certain general life cycles through which your career passes. These include the following.

During your twenties you are laying the foundation of your career. You are learning the functions of the job, the work habits and the organizational culture which lets you perform to your full capacity. You are also developing the friends and lifestyle which may stay with you for life.

In your thirties you will begin to assert yourself and go forward with your career. You are accustomed to relating to your bosses and your peers, and to evaluating their perceptions of you.

You are into overdrive in your forties. You have begun the experience of being boss and giving orders and are less able to take orders from others. Now you should be at decision-making level – your reports cause change rather than just giving advice. Promotions from now on happen less often but are more significant.

When you blossom into your fifties, your reputation will have gone ahead of you. You will be consolidating your skills and using your achievements to your best advantage. You get through work quickly, are accustomed to leading and not only are you learning more but you will want to *earn* even more. You are being paid for what you have done – the company wants your commitment.

Depending on your success to date, you can use your sixties either to retire and indulge in your hobbies, or continue on the upward track. Many are still active and growing in influence while others at this stage enjoy the role of being the *éminence grise*.

At some stage you will reach a make or break point and your state of progress will slow down or accelerate from there. This transition period, and how you deal with it, is the key to success in your career. You will determine your own status by your level of acceptance of yourself as special, and by proving this to others – you will have increased your influence through friends who are also going places.

The faults which might derail you include personality traits and habits which annoy. However, the defects which, if strong and persistent, can cause you long-term trouble come into four main categories:

1. Over-confidence. This includes bad habits such as talking all the time. One day it could lead to you not being promoted, or being left out of a project, because your colleagues have had enough.
2. Being over-demanding. This can lead you into the trap of telling others how good you are, that you know best, and that your way is the only way. Let your achievements speak for themselves, rather than justifying your existence constantly.
3. Being a doom and gloomster. There is always one person who prophesies trouble, who always sees problems and who demotivates colleagues who may be over-enthusiastic but who do not need to be always reined in. This behaviour can sidetrack you from mainstream projects, no matter how competent you are, because of the effect you have on others.
4. Being a loner. Not wanting to be part of the team is a frequent attitude of those with a specific or technical skill. By showing that you are really not interested in the general management system, you could be destined to stay at middle management level.

The qualities you will need at all stages in your life – both professional and personal – are qualities which translate into business success.

Honesty and integrity always come top of the list as reasons why corporations and people want to be associated with, and be staffed by, those who are known to have these qualities.

A close second is maturity – this is not related to age alone, but to qualities of judgment and behaviour. By knowing when to delegate, when to listen to experts and when to rule the roost, you will show your mature attitudes.

Thoughtfulness for others' feelings and the talent for making people comfortable are priceless qualities to possess. Yet a degree of stubbornness – or a healthy determination not to give up – will help see you through awkward projects and difficult relationships. Inflexibility is not always appropriate, but where you use it to win it is entirely valid. It is a great aid when you need to assert yourself.

Mental toughness is learnt from hard experience. Using your self-discipline constructively, keeping your mind focused on the job in hand, and not letting emotions interfere, gives you an advantage over those of a weaker mentality. You will give clear signals for others to understand and resolve situations more easily.

Think through all the issues in this chapter and decide whether you need to change any aspects of your life-style, working practices, attitudes and your motivation. Everything about you can be put into the melting pot – only you can do this and only you can ensure that the shape that emerges is one that you like, know and wish others to know and respect.

· 2 ·

Building Your Reputation

Your pattern of development depends primarily on your self-esteem, as the following diagram demonstrates:

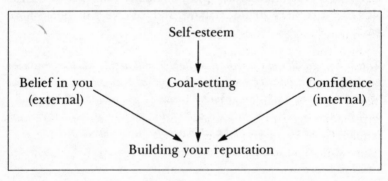

Self-esteem

Belief in you   Goal-setting   Confidence
(external)   (internal)

Building your reputation

Your appreciation of self-worth is based on your security, success and experience. By knowing what you can do and how you can improve, you will progress, and you can do this by learning, asking, and observing. For example, have you worked out who is doing best in your office? How is this determined? By the number of clients, production, profit margins achieved? Have you discovered how the 'best' person has built up the reputation – is it based on results or is it that the person is *perceived* to be 'doing well'? The two may not match when analysed (which is more important?).

It is tempting to believe that building your professional reputation depends on mastering certain social and technical skills and behaviours. Important as these are, they represent only the tip of the ice-berg of all the qualities and traits which mark you out for success. If you are truly committed to achieving your full potential, you need to start your quest at a deeper level – you need to examine your emotions and attitudes before you can move on to behaviours and skills. How well you perform, how well you respond to change and new challenges is determined by your most profound sense of *who* you are. Equipping yourself with self-esteem is a vital step along the road to growth and development. Understanding yourself better is a liberating process which will ensure you will realize your full potential.

This chapter examines how you need *consciously* to develop a balanced and mature sense of self-worth. It goes on to explore the vital role that emotions play in energizing you to fulfill your needs and keep growing as an individual. Developing a better sense of self-worth and understanding how you can take control of your personal growth will give you new freedom and power.

Once you reach this point, you will then be ready to begin considering how to use that freedom and power to achieve success in your job and career. You need to recognize the inner needs that drive your motivation; eg is security and comfort more important to you than the praise and respect of colleagues and family? Once you unravel these issues you will know what you really want. You will be able to formulate specific learning goals and long-term career plans. You can make *choices* because you know where you want to go.

Finally, the chapter ends at what might have seemed to some as the starting point of building a professional reputation – how to position yourself so that you can ensure being at the right place at the right time. This section explores the type of image you want to cultivate; how to gain recognition; and how to project your appearance to both your colleagues and your clients.

Perhaps the most important message of this chapter is that you have inside you vital resources and strengths which you need to access if you are to be fully successful. Embark on an inner voyage before you take your company or profession by storm. You will find it is well worth the effort.

2.1 DEVELOPING SELF-ESTEEM

Self-esteem grows with practice. It is an aspect of personality which needs to be nurtured consciously and carefully so that it exerts a beneficial, liberating influence in a person's life and is not a barrier preventing him or her from grasping new opportunities and challenges. Not everyone will be able easily to subscribe to this view of self-esteem. British culture, for example, encourages people to put others first and to minimize their own wants. This is fine, as long as they have learnt to look at themselves and like what they see. In the USA, however, it is far more acceptable to say 'I am' or 'I want', and to discuss self-worth with all and sundry from an early age. But it is only by *consciously* assessing your own abilities and competencies that you can recognize how far you have travelled and where you next want to go in your personal and career development.

It is important to recognize that self-esteem and the ability to change and develop are inextricably linked. The ability to change comes only when a person grows in maturity and begins to develop a balanced understanding of their worth. Charles Handy, and other management gurus like Tom Peters and Robert Heller, made 'Management for Change' the clarion call for business in the 1980s. Make a similar commitment in your own personal life. Recognize that personal growth depends on adjusting, accepting and enabling change to happen.

Remember, however, that adapting to change also requires the willingness to take control. Only by being secure in yourself, can you go on to take responsibility for your actions, and then to take control and influence the outcome of those actions. This may or may not involve other people, but it will have a simple effect in the workplace: you will be seen as someone who is both willing and able to undertake more and more onerous tasks.

The challenge for personal growth then, involves three key

factors: consciously developing a realistic, balanced sense of self-worth; being open to change; and being willing and able to take control.

Begin the process of developing right now by reviewing your past development – you will almost certainly find that past experiences have taught you a surprising range of skills. This exercise will help you to see that personal growth occurs in small, seemingly insignificant stages. Then, when you achieve your next step forward, you will recognize your progress and your self-esteem will grow accordingly.

Step-by-step growth

When you were growing up, you probably had to join in with family chores and interact in the family group. You are probably known to your parents and siblings for being 'good at' something: anything from baby-sitting to mending fuses, from making the best coffee cake to having a sense of colour in decoration. Do not dismiss these skills as trivial but instead consider them as part of your overall competency. Consider in more detail the abilities which underly these achievements; for example organizational and time management skills.

In school/college days, were you a sports captain, committee chairman, campaigner or any such prominent person? Did you take charge of the art cupboard or cleaning of the playground perhaps? Did you arrange the College Ball? Did you make sure that friends knew where to meet for a party? Leadership and social skills acquired when growing up are carried on through life and are added to by each event and experience in which you are involved. The most apparently insignificant responsibility can become a valuable tool in knowing how to take charge at another time.

If you have spent time in institutional or service life, you will have had the experience of living and working in a hierarchy where everyone has an allocated position and taskbase. This can be a useful insight into responsibility and the roles of leader and follower. In corporate life there is a similarly recognizable structure of responsibility. Working within such structures requires learning certain roles and behaviours. Rather than ignoring or resisting hierarchy, you can learn to grow within it and, by understanding and using organizational systems, develop further.

Once you embark on your chosen career, you will learn different, perhaps more subtle, forms of responsibility. These include the following:

- There will be times when you are in a position to receive or give favours. This type of responsibility is fragile and requires careful handling. Remember that if you choose to enter into such arrangements, you must take full responsibility for the outcome.
- A more intangible but vital responsibility is to accept and embrace risk. Fear can affect your decision making or the way you carry out tasks. You may be constrained to be as inconspicuous as possible and not seek further responsibilities because you are vulnerable. You may be afraid to take risks because you need money to meet your needs, or you may be afraid of failing to meet the expectations of your superiors. This is a difficult problem: by not taking chances and not accepting responsibility you interfere with your self-esteem, and will plateau or regress rather than going on and achieving. Confront the fear, analyse the causes and negate the effects by taking action.
- Closely allied to the need to accept risk is your responsibility always to seek new or creative approaches to your job. Following the tradition or practice of others without checking the validity of your actions will not necessarily allow you to take control. Just because something has always been done in a certain way, it does not necessarily have to go on like that. This is part of the ability to change, but it is even more vital when keeping or acquiring control. The risk is that your plan or idea might not be accepted at the time, and you must be prepared for this. Occasionally, you may have to take the blame for a flop or a disgruntled client. Provided this is not a regular occurrence, you should be able to analyse the causes, deal with the problem as a matter of course and limit the damage. By

facing up to the crisis, explaining (without overdoing the self-justification) to seniors and remedying the situation, you may be recognized as a valuable manager. Dealing with the dilemma 'up front' rather than letting it fester is strongly recommended. 'If I forget it, it will go away', is a dangerous attitude.

Being able to 'think on your feet' is a vital component of taking responsibility. Learn to respond calmly and effectively to unexpected phone calls, meetings, circumstances, etc.

You need self-worth, self-love, self-acceptance and the freedom to be the unique and unrepeatable person you are. You need to be touched and mirrored by those around you. You need a structure within which it is safe enough to risk growth and become even more individual. Such a structure will change according to the stages of your development, and at all stages you need affection and recognition and to have your feelings affirmed. You will also need stimulation and challenges in order to move on and develop; to establish your self-esteem.

Harnessing emotions

The power to feel allows you to know your own unique spontaneous reality. You have the tools, the emotions, to allow you to be fully aware of where you are in fulfilling your needs. Emotions are 'energy in motion', or a type of nervous energy, and allow you to prepare to meet and resolve any threat to your basic needs. This is the process through which you can uphold your dignity and self-esteem. The major emotions are as follows:

Fear This allows you to assess danger and to be conscious of danger zones when establishing yourself and developing.

Sadness This includes 'completing' actions, such as saying goodbye. Life is a continuous cycle of hellos and goodbyes, of finishing off cycles of growth.

Grief When acknowledged and gone through, this gives you the ability to round off the past. Saying goodbye to certain periods of your life is part of growing up and becoming an adult. Grief is the healing feeling.

Guilt This is the energy which forms your conscience. You need this unpleasant but healthy feeling to keep your sensitivities alive. (Without sensitivity you may have mental health problems.) Guilt in its most positive sense allows you to stand for something and to have an internal value system that makes it possible for you to commit yourself to certain actions and behaviours.

Shame This lets you know that you are limited and finite. It gives you permission to make mistakes and also lets you know when you need to seek help.

Joy This signals to you that all is well; that your needs are being met and that you are alive and thriving. It makes you feel full of new and boundless energy.

You have the power to want and desire – this is your volition, your will, your ability to choose. Your will is the power of your desire raised to the intensity of action. Your choices shape your reality and your life.

The ability to imagine gives you the opportunity to look into new and different spheres of activity. Without imagination, you would become a conformist, following the example of others. Imagination gives you hope, optimism and creativity.

Some psychologists believe that we are born with a deep and profound sense of worth which develops or is stunted according to the good or bad caretaking done by parents or guardians when we are growing up. To continue to feel precious and unique, we have to feel the preciousness and uniqueness mirrored in our parents' eyes. However, reputation today may be founded in the early years but now, as an adult, you are free to take control.

Your freedoms are:

To live in the present. This means seeing and hearing what is here and now, rather than what was, will be or should be.

To think what you think rather than what you should think.

To feel what you feel rather than what you should feel.

To want or desire what you choose rather than what you should want or desire.

To imagine your individuality rather than playing it safe and conforming.

These freedoms add up to your full self-acceptance and integration. You will have enormous personal power resulting from accepting these freedoms. All your energies will be free to flow outward in order to cope with the world, giving you freedom to function well.

2.2 SETTING GOALS

In setting the goals leading to planning your career, you need to discover what you are capable of doing well and what you could develop further by training, education or work experience. Graduate training schemes now include a broad range of activities spread over as many companies as possible so that you can find out what it would be like to pursue several different careers before making your choice. It is more difficult to find such an opportunity once you are in a job.

Many companies now provide continuous development programmes for managers in order to aid the 'self-directed, lifelong learning' precept encouraged by so many leading training specialists. After making sure that your company provides such programmes, it is up to you to make yourself available. You need access to both general and skills training to maximize the effectiveness of the time you will be spending on your self-development.

If your company will not send you to workshops, seminars or sessions, you can develop yourself using books, distance-learning manuals and through attending evening or weekend courses given by interest groups or professional associations.

Your values and expectations will be influenced by the way you were brought up and by your home and school experiences. When candidates are selected for senior posts, just as much time is spent discussing their early life and what their results at school and college show as in discussing their present responsibilities. This is because together they indicate *growth*.

The winning side of an individual usually shows early, as does the influence of the highly motivated parent/teacher or relative/ friend. Everything you do is the result of both universal and specific factors. Just as the level of nutrition you had when young affects your physical growth, so the input from your surroundings affects your knowledge and ambition. For example, those with professional parents often follow the same career because they know how to achieve within that framework and are familiar with the effort required, as well as having contacts who make it more accessible. Conversely, you may decide that what your parents are doing is exactly what you do not want to do, and look for something entirely different. Either way, you have been motivated positively. It is much harder for you if you have not had such continuous role models, due to the absence of close relatives or constant adult companions, and you should be admired if you have nevertheless succeeded and reached your goal completely by using any help you have been able to find.

Maslow has argued that goals are not static but that they alter as the individual seeks 'higher' forms of fulfilment. You will know how your goals have changed over the years, in different companies, the level of your ambition being based on your responsibilities at the time, or on your relationship with colleagues or others who are important in your life at any particular stage. So your goals, and their order of priority, will always be in a state of flux. This does not matter – the important thing is to have goals, and to review them regularly.

The following section looks at some of the major goals and desires that drive people and influence their career choices. Consider whether and how you fit into any of these categories.

Comfort goals

The largest and most variable group of goals is that labelled 'security', or 'comfort'. These may revolve around a desired lifestyle or they may simply aim to ensure a roof over one's head.

The basic needs of food, drink and shelter are only superseded when they are easily acquired. Then you set goals for the *way* in which you can cater for these needs.

Depending on your background and ability, your goals will vary from, say, being a plumber to having a seat on the Board. The higher up the ladder you climb, the lower the level of discomfort in your lifestyle is likely to be, but your need for more comfort will probably be greater. Keeping up with the Joneses is an old-fashioned concept now, but you may still want a better house, car, schooling for the children, etc. This means that there is always a degree of stress at every career level, because you are trying to achieve goals which extend beyond the immediate possibility.

If you are concerned with 'comfort' goals more than anything else, you are more likely to settle for jobs with security; perhaps involving repetitive processes, regular money and minimal stress. You can discover how important these goals are for yourself by asking some basic questions. Are you so settled that you would be unwilling to relocate? Are you unwilling to participate in sports in case you get hurt? Are you well covered by insurance in case of illness? If you answer these questions positively, this indicates that you have a preoccupation with comfort and are willing to settle for easily achievable goals.

People who pursue comfort goals can also be high achievers. Such individuals may want a lifestyle catering for comfort, but are willing to suffer on the way to acquiring this. They fully expect to end up with what they want, but they have discovered that they want more than can be won by stopping at the present level. Whether they are obsessed by big money, by winning at sports, owning the Rolls, or whether they want to prove their abilities, they are less impressed by the goods and chattels of comfort than by the exhilaration of achievement and by the recognition of others. Do either of these types of people describe you?

Financial goals

For many people, the importance of financial goals fluctuates according to macro economic trends. At times when a basic level of prosperity seems assured people view other goals, such as self-development, as more important. But the more uncertain the economic climate, the more important financial security becomes. You need to consider how important financial success is to you, then structure your goal–setting accordingly.

Individuals who seek financial security are likely to seek a structured life as a means of continuing certain satisfactory experiences. For some people, however, achieving financial well-being is a means of escaping from certain unhappy experiences. Is this something that drives you? It may have bred in them a strong need to find a safe and secure lifestyle. These people may find that achieving financial goals requires greater effort due to the need to fight against those negative influences.

Anyone who is strongly motivated by financial security should be aware that other people can use this to manipulate them. There have always been employers or organizations who have used threats of insecurity as a method of controlling employees. The threat of the sack, isolation, or uncertainty about promotion are all involved to some degree wherever you work. The latter is probably the most usual barrier to recognize you will face. However, an increasing 'threat' is now coming from the growing number of mergers, acquisitions, and management and leveraged buyouts. If you are working for a company which has been taken over, you need to recognize the need for adjustment. The positive way to deal with this is to regard it as another platform from which to view what you want, to look at your performance requirements in the new company and to set new goals accordingly. It is another chance to make your mark and to find your niche in a new structure.

People motivated by financial goals either love or hate structure. The former will tend to be attracted to services, big banks, public sector and insurance companies. These people like to know that their work routine will never be greatly disturbed.

The absolute opposite of the structured profile is to be found in the entrepreneur. The thriving small business sector in many Western economies bears testament to the growing number of people motivated by the desire for independence and freedom from structure and hierarchy (as well as the obvious desire to get rich quick!). So if you don't like working within boundaries, within a strict hierarchy or routine bureaucratic regime, then go elsewhere – you will not shine within the limits of that type of organization. There is always a place for the intrapreneur (the entrepreneur within an organization), but this is usually someone who finds scope within the structure, rather than an entrepreneur looking for a career.

You will benefit from trying as many jobs as possible when you first qualify, until you find a congenial environment or have enough experience to 'do your own thing'. There has been a great increase in understanding of enterprise and small businesses during the last decade, so you will find help to go in that direction and make your name that way. You should recognize your need for immediate feedback by direct rewards – the scale of the operation will not matter so much for you at the beginning as will the signs of early profit making. You should give yourself attainable goals frequently in order to achieve them quickly.

Recognition and status goals

You may need recognition from the company within which you work, or seek external recognition. You may need to manage and control others in order to build your recognition and reputation. In either case, you should set goals that meet your needs and achieve your objectives. The self-esteem you are developing should now be strong enough for you to understand the cause and effect of *yourself* in your career positioning.

By accepting punishment or reward as the end result of behaviour, you will have been conditioned by the emphasis placed during the time you were growing up, and now you will be facing the same in a more subtle form in your job. It is no longer higher or lower marks, being sent to your room or getting a present; now it is bonus payments and promotions based on performance.

You may react well to being rewarded and, as with comfort goals, be looking for quick recognition. By joining a highly-structured system such as the professions or the services, you will have these needs satisfied.

If working under threat of demolition, management by fear or constant checking is how you operate best then find a company with traditional (often family) management, or a public company tightly accountable to the Board/shareholders in a volatile market. The City, since 'Big Bang', comes under this heading. Many people were making big money one day and went bankrupt the next. Not all have survived to tell the tale, opting for a quiet life elsewhere rather than persevering in that environment. You may need considerably energy, not to say courage, to continue high-level performance in this type of environment. The same is also true for the entrepreneur risking all on the next big deal, the property developer about to close after five years planning and risk-takers who await public accolade or the bankruptcy court.

Blocking and unblocking

Learning from experience is fine, where the job gives you the chance to innovate, experiment and learn from mistakes, but often this only occurs when you change your job, or job content. Promotion is the most obvious way of increasing experience through responsibility, getting to know a new set of colleagues and reporting to a different level of decision-makers.

Job rotation (a method of training) gives you access to different functions and responses. Similarly, when tasks are added to your existing job, you get a chance to show your adaptability and competence. Secondment, a useful practice of the Civil Service for some time, is becoming more widespread. Now larger companies are spreading expertise by lending managers to other enterprises, e.g. to training schemes, small businesses and educational institutes. This can be a way for you to shine, so do not hesitate too long if you are offered secondment. Special projects or one-off openings can be added to your normal routine. It is becoming more and more acceptable to be a working member of a committee, an internal task force or temporary project, or a charity. All these could give you some valuable new experience.

Are you subject to a corporate culture which lacks a training ethos? Have you accepted this and decided that it is not worth the effort to find training for yourself outside working hours? Think again. Why not give yourself the necessary aids to being even better at your job? Take the risk – what you lost in confidence by being idiosyncratic, you will balance by using your new knowhow.

Blockages against learning/training are common. A bad experience may inhibit someone from embarking on further training. Time spent at school, college or other learning establishments may not have achieved its objectives for you. You may not have 'learned how to learn' and given up. There is always time to remedy this, even if your boss is not particularly supportive. It is up to you – take the risk. Opportunities will arise if you go looking, and your communication skills will improve with knowledge, making you more able to tell others what you are actually aiming to do.

You should make plans for:

- Reviewing your present skills against your future goals
- Analysing your learning style
- Identifying what you need to do to perform better
- Setting standards of performance – how do you work best?
- Initiating the openings to acquire information/training

By listening, accepting help, sharing with others and checking your achievements, you will find it easier to take risks. Then you can help your colleagues and staff to increase their performance too, and increase your influence in other spheres.

The case of Diana Cornish, Managing Director of Brook Street employment agency, should encourage you to commit yourself to self-development. Diana left school without any exam-passes. She worked as a receptionist in her grandfather's factory and learned shorthand and typing at evening classes, then went to work as a costings accounts clerk while still working part-time for her grandfather. Although she had a new baby, she became an Avon lady in the evenings. This led to managing 200 representatives, which prepared her for her appointment as training manager for Blue Arrow Group where she became Regional Director. In 1985 Blue Arrow bought Brook Street and in 1986 she was appointed as MD. Now in the early 1990s she has been leading a management buy-out.

Diana has high personal motivation, and this can be something that you too can have. She wanted to do better than anyone else and still has ambitions waiting to be realized.

You can achieve as long as you know what you want to do. 'It's no good thinking that you are ordinary. Everybody is special and everybody has got something special about them,' says Diana. She maintains that you look for the best possible jobs with the best possible money and then learn as fast as you can to gain the expertise. She had to fight to get what she wanted because it was not easily on offer. Make sure you are not in the wrong job – if you are, move now.

2.3 CAREER PLANNING

Company environment

Consider the company you are working for now. Can you visualize yourself in the same conditions in five to ten years time? What would you like to be doing then? Currently, only 13 per cent of senior people run their own businesses but this is increasing. Those of you who have moved into self-employment (29 per cent) will be employees in large companies now; about 33 per cent of you are in medium-sized companies. You are looking for job satisfaction, challenge and personal self-fulfilment through taking the risk of becoming an entrepreneur.

Most of you (59 per cent) were in your twenties when you became interested in being managers. Those of you who became interested after your first promotion are some 48 per cent; and ten per cent had visions of management while you were still at school. You give ambition and the work itself as the reasons for having control at work and input into decision-making. The need to achieve results, meet challenges and seek new opportunities have been the strongest influences on your progress. About 80 per cent of you admit to being happy in your work in management, but 70 per cent would like to be involved in top management strategy, and 61 per cent to have further training in information technology.

This survey (Korn/Ferry International, 1987) gives some fascinating insights into the factors which influence people's career progress – it also reveals how rarely they resort to any form of career planning. Many people are resistant to the idea of life-planning and setting goals. It is not part of early educational training, so there is little experience of its benefits at an early age. It can be easier to accept the status quo and proceed on an ad hoc basis rather than to look at yourself and examine the possibilities, potential and desires which lead to goal-setting.

Are you so busy getting by from day to day that you have not considered the next steps in your career and in your life in general? It is essential to take responsibility for yourself and try to lessen your dependence on others and on events as they happen. The act of planning is part of a greater move to becoming responsible for yourself.

In order to do the things which will enhance or enrich your life in some way you must be aware that you cannot separate your work life from your personal life. Both involve the same person – you – what you do in one area will affect what happens in another sphere.

Now is as good a time as any to start planning. Begin by describing your life today, very briefly: your personal life and your work life. How satisfied are you? Is anything changing in your life? What are the components? Your work? Your relationships? You? Where is the pressure to change coming from? The situation? Other people? If so, who? Or is it coming from you? What changes do you want *now* in your life?

Face the real implications of what is happening, and what the outcomes will be if you continue in your present mode. To help jog your memory and to clarify your attitudes, thoughts and abilities, here are some trigger questions to get you to consider the original sources of those aspects, as well as helping to recall past ambitions and needs. (Short answers are enough to get you thinking.):

1. What was the high point of last week?
2. Who is the one person most responsible for making you what you are today?
3. What is the riskiest decision you have ever made? Why was the risk so great?

4. Which individual do you admire most?
5. When you were a young child, what did you want to grow up to be?
6. If you were suddenly told you had six months to live, what would you do in that time?

Take your answers and draw a line representing your life on a large piece of paper. Start with birth and childhood, where you are as an adult, then where you will go in the future. Give yourself an imaginary yardstick and draw the line up and down, showing the ups and downs you have been through, including the significant people and events. Be as creative as you like – this exercise incorporates your past, present and future. You should be able to visualize patterns as they emerge and get a better idea of why you are where you are today. Then you will be better prepared to plan the changes you have to make to reach your goals.

Individual contribution

Allow yourself a brain-storming session (sharing with others is a good idea here). Take a piece of paper and write a list of all the things you are able to do – and that means *everything* you are capable of doing. Do not censor anything, even the washing-up or changing a tyre, because even the so-called 'little things' matter; everything you do is applicable to work. Then discuss the list with someone who knows you well enough to remind you of what you have forgotten.

Now you can be impressed by yourself: all those things you have been doing, often by habit or without thinking about them, are skills and can be applied in different ways, including better use of them at work. You will begin to see your strengths and weaknesses emerging. Do not undervalue your worth.

When you have remembered the past and collected your resources, the object is to move into the future. Start fantasizing about what you could do if you had complete freedom and no restrictions to prevent you from proceeding. Relaxation techniques like the following are helpful in getting the brain floating into the future and seeing yourself in action:

1. Sit in a comfortable position and close your eyes.
2. Make sure you are warm, comfortable and unlikely to be disturbed. (Soft lights and music make a good background setting.)
3. Take a deep breath and relax.

Now, start imagining yourself walking into the future. Mentally leave the room and visualize a place where you would like to be. It is seven years later. Where are you? You are standing outside the place you want to live in – go through the door. What does it look like? Is it a town or country? Is it a familiar place? A grand place? Is it bare or complete?

Look at the details – style of furnishing, fireplace fittings, colours, collections, the door handle, the food in the kitchen, the flowers in the window. Is there a garden? Walk around all the rooms. Is there a vehicle outside? Smell the atmosphere. Are you alone? Who else is there? What are they doing?

To achieve the standard of living you have visualized, what do you have to earn or do? Where have you come in from? Who (if anyone) shares your life? Is this important?

Is this a totally different scene from today? Is it the same? How old are you? How old are the people around you?

Now, do the same from your place of work. What sort of operation is going on? What is your position? What is your influence? Are you happy? What more do you want to do? Write down these scenarios – then work out your goal-setting to achieve your fantasy.

After setting your seven-year objectives, make a five-year plan, then break it down so that you understand your year-by-year, step-by-step goals. Include work-related goals, personal goals and some just for fun. Then share what you are planning with those who can give you support and encouragement at any time. Those who will be affected by your plans can also be included, if you wish, so that they will be more understanding of the changes you will be making. When obstacles arise, do not give up, but think of ways of getting around them.

Choices

The right place
When you have sorted out your career goals you will be able to choose the right position for the next step. Choosing the function, company, boss and whatever else you can control gives you an edge on your competitors.

Picking a job
Your jobs should be *selected*, not accepted (even first ones). Begin by selecting a *career* you would enjoy (each *job* may not be enjoyable). It is almost impossible to succeed in business if you don't like your work.

Picking an industry
By the time you are 30, you should have decided what industry you want to be in – and be in it. When you are picking your industry, take a broad view of it to figure out what industry you are really in. Check that the values within that sector match your own where possible.

Picking a speciality
The fastest route to the top in the corporate world changes almost from year to year. In 1979, for instance, it was finance and accounting; in 1988 it was marketing; human resource management is predicted to be the key route in the early 1990s.

However, unless simply getting to the top is your only goal, your choice of route should not be wholly governed by such trends.

Choosing a company
Career choices made quite early in your working life can be decisive in determining its course. For instance, it is more difficult to move between industries after you are 30 because senior appointments call for a deep knowledge of the company's main line of business. No matter how successful your track-record is, it is hard to cross over to another kind of industry later in life.

The crucial choice you have to make at the early stages in your working life, therefore, is the size of the organization you join. Executive search consultant, Andrew Garner of Boyden International, believes that: 'When looking for a first-division player, you'll probably extend the search to the second division but not the fourth. A candidate from the fourth division may be very talented but is used to playing the game at a different pace and at a different level of competition.' Size is, of course, relative to each industry: some sectors proliferate large scale organizations, others do not.

Big companies are generally not interested in the small-company generalist who has been immersed in detail. Big companies want strategic thinkers who can get things done, so it is easier to move from the big to the small. Better training facilities in larger organizations mean that joining Mars, Proctor & Gamble or IBM early in your career will make you well-prepared for big or small companies.

The smaller the company you are in, the greater will be your influence – but you are expected to do more tasks yourself in a small company and may not be able to recruit your own staff. Peter Drucker and Tom Peters both believe that the small company experience has been underestimated. The move towards decentralized units, task forces and project teams to replace hierarchical structures will mean that more and more top management jobs in big companies will be filled by luring people away from smaller ones.

Corporate culture is something else to consider. Do the values and image of the company match your own? If not, could you adapt accordingly, and happily? Make sure that the end result suits your career plan.

Remember that however carefully you make your choices, your success will also depend on a certain amount of luck, for example, being in the right place at the right time or being noticed by the person who can offer you promotion.

However, in the case of almost every successful person, luck was a necessary but not a sufficient condition for his or her success. As Machiavelli said: 'Without those individuals' own powers, their opportunities would have come in vain'. Be prepared to make the most of an opportunity when it arises.

2.4 VISIBILITY

Positioning yourself

Start well. Go to the best company you can find in 'your' sector, or at least to a firm of professional calibre which is appropriate to your aims. With the recent demographic shift, the choice may well be yours at the stage of the university 'milk-round'. It is no longer usual to start with one company and stay there for life – moving sideways and ever upwards is more likely to be your path.

Nobody has an easy time getting to the top. Nobody admits that is where they are aiming until they are nearly there. Be sure that you are prepared for the struggles at the critical points in your career which will inevitably happen. As a future senior executive, are you, for example, prepared to be mobile; to recognize and seize opportunities as they arise, however inconvenient they may appear?

You will reach key points in your career where you must make the right moves to propel yourself into senior management. Those who stumble at these points are often just as bright and hardworking as those who succeed, but they have neglected to make the most of their assets and have failed to position themselves correctly for future development. If you fail to reach the top, the fault will not be the state of the economy – it will be yourself. You will get good jobs (part of your career strategy) if you are the best possible candidate for those jobs.

Working out your ultimate goal is time well spent – even if it takes several years. Practise looking up from your own little patch and getting the global view. (This is sometimes called the 'helicopter approach'.) Learning to see as much as possible of the big picture that is your life in order to recognize the pieces and how they fit together. Women are particularly prone to being task-orientated – keeping involved with the immediate rather than long-term or overall implications. This 'bigger view' will help increase your independence, because by stopping, thinking and planning, you gain control over your situation, rather than reacting constantly to urgent requirements.

A cautionary note: you must accept, even at this early stage, that it is impossible to separate personal life from working life – both have to be considered when planning. Life is made up of everything you are involved in; you will be affected in one sphere by what is happening in another.

What sort of image should you cultivate? The 1988–89 results analysed in *Planning for Social Change* by the Henley Centre for Forecasting reveals that the British admire people who are hard-working, self-confident and healthy, rather than those who are rich, sporty and ostentatious. People who take time for leisure, sitting in the sunshine, watching TV and generally taking life easily are regarded as self-indulgent and unimpressive. Self-confidence, ambition and modesty are the highest-valued personality and physical traits, followed by social competence in the form of intelligence and the ability to speak, dress and entertain well. The strongest influences in people's lives are perceived to be a) the partner or spouse, b) children and c) friends and parents.

If you want instant acclaim, you will be attracted to jobs where money is closely related to performance and where you can show your success in having the latest car, travel, friends, night life, etc. This is different from building your reputation, but may be part of the method you employ. High profile people do, of course, get noticed. The disadvantage of highly public reputations is that they rise *and fall* publicly.

What sort of financial rewards are you looking for? You may be able to perform better when your results are clearly rewarded immediately, and therefore want a career where performance is regularly measured and paid for. If, on the other hand, you want long-term security, then look for a career based on a high pension and rights at the end of a long, steady career.

You will find that recognition goals recede in importance in times of family emergencies – at such times, the comfort goals increase in importance. Even if you are a high achiever, you will want to know that your daily needs are easily met when there is illness, or when a disabled child or suchlike enters into consideration.

Your desire for status and approbation needs to be strong enough for you to continue when such responsibilities are involved. If you are to be a recognized success, a person with a reputation for achievement, then you may have to face difficult choices. If others, such as a partner, are involved then it becomes even more complex. So the need for determination to succeed has to be strong. The nature of your work and the company you are doing it for will affect this: flexi-time, compassionate leave, career breaks and so on, all make it easier for you to deal with emergencies.

It is now established that high achievers report ill infrequently: they are less interested in their illnesses than those at lower levels. This is partly due to the determination just discussed, and partly to the focus on the tasks involved in reaching the goals they have set. Check your situation: if you have a pattern of sick days, either it is a symptom of the job not supplying enough challenges, or you have a physical problem which needs help. Either way, it may be a good time to review your goals and think about whether you need to change your present priorities.

Realizing ambition

For most jobs, companies are looking for ambitious, strong, self-motivated people who will take themselves and the company onwards and upwards. However, most people are not ambitious, or so they say. In *Unique Success Propositions*, Robert Heller maintains that in any group of managers the majority will deny ambition. When quizzed about their entrepreneurial qualities – including high but realistic and achievable goals, belief that they can control their own fates and a high level of drive and energy – the result is largely dismissive.

So is your potential for success stifled by yourself or by your environment? Day-dreaming like Walter Mitty about the fame and success which really is beyond daily grasp is self-defeating, but if, like most people, you are in danger of achieving relatively little of your imagined potential, it can be psychologically convenient to deny ever having had the desire. Perhaps your environment is holding you back. It is hard to be personally successful within a failing organization, so look for an environment within which you can grow. Heller suggests asking yourself the following questions when considering joining an organization:

1. In what techniques is the company better than others?

2. What markets does it know better?
3. Where are its powers of creative thinking and innovations better?
4. Where is its operating/productive proficiency better?
5. Where is it more effective in driving forward new enterprises and creating new wealth?

Then check where you would fit in and grow within the group.

It is unusual for companies to ask these questions and they can end up like you when you falsely believe that you lack entrepreneurial qualities – when all you really need is the incentive to achieve. There is more to success than just wanting it – you (and the company) need leadership, challenge, decisiveness, speed, clarity, mastery of the basics, firm objectives and acceptance of change: the eight attributes which Heller calls the sustaining principles. They are all capable of development, and both your personal ambition and the corporate entrepreneurial success will thrive on a success-driven, supportive and sustaining environment backed up with acceptance and training.

These new attitudes have, to some extent, been accompanied by corresponding corporate promotion practices. In almost every industry upward mobility is accepted and encouraged. Promotions come more quickly – so are you in a job where this is happening? Any edge you can get might be the edge that gets you the job.

Doing your job well is necessary, getting recognition for it is essential. Those who reach the top have been calculating in their careers. They look at themselves and think: 'How can I market this? What is interesting about my career? Who is interested in it? How can I get my message across?'

You cannot start merchandizing yourself too soon, *and you should never stop.* Making the effort to make positive impressions should be a lifelong habit. Career breakdowns crop up unpredictably, and jobs will go to those who have made themselves ready to be promoted. Developing, spotting and labelling talent is hyperorganized, involving evaluation, appraisal, high-flier programmes, etc, but normally one or two people emerge clearly. What signs does your company look for? Who makes it into the 'watch' list? Getting noticed early on demands the following considerations:

- The way you think, eg quickly acquiring appropriate skills, is a learnt habit
- Working hard, eg after hours, early in the morning, etc, is only noteworthy if you are producing extra business by doing it
- Performance – financial results will aid you in being considered worthy of promotion. No matter how 'good' your results are, if they do not have a financial plus factor for the company they are of little value
- Motivating people – having people skills will give you the wherewithal to build your team, department, division, etc. This leads to seniority
- Common sense is always an asset, never a liability
- Courage is a definite requirement, no matter what level you find yourself at

People who reach the top take advantage of every minute. They do what they have to do – and then they do more.

> *'He has trouble getting on with people. To me that is the kiss of death.'* Lee Iacocca.

Likability – getting along with people in an atmosphere of mutual success is vastly underrated as an element of corporate success.

There is a natural element in likability, but there can be a calculated component as well. It is in your interest to make sure that certain people like you, and you should make the effort to see that they do. This applies not only to your superiors, but also to your peers, who may be your subordinates one day. Learn to:

- Approach people openly and honestly
- Avoid obvious flattery (maturity is being able to handle people)
- Avoid false claims to common interests
- Be actually likable

- Apologize with explanation only when you have no alternative

2.5 GAINING RECOGNITION

When establishing yourself in an organization you need to be easily recognizable. Suggestions for achieving this include:

- Have a trademark, habit or phrase that people associate with you
- Cultivate your idiosyncrasies for the same reason
- Keep a sense of humour – it is all right to laugh at yourself
- Be positive – optimism is a magnet to other people
- Love yourself – then others will love you too
- Looking good is not to be underestimated
- Be assertive – uncertainty and indecision loses friends and followers
- Realize that it's OK to say 'I don't know' – but not too often
- Make money – keep it and share what it buys at the same time

You show your charisma when you are seen to be:

- A born persuader
- Dynamic and active
- A confident speaker
- A frequent user of hand gestures
- Alert in your body language
- Easily believed

Do you fit into the category of not being able to be bought or caught? If you do, you are in charge of yourself and give out positive signals.

Being *seen* to be competent/friendly/promotable should rarely involve *saying* that you are competent/friendly/promotable, etc. Keep the mystery. You will know if you've got what it takes by other's responses. Your reputation can be harmed by: following fashions/using status symbols, overdrinking, grumbling, silly behaviour, taking life too seriously or being a stereotype. It can be enriched by: being invited to significant events, getting high on personality, forgiving and being forgiven, having the last laugh, doing something in a light manner and having style.

Looking the part

Whether you like it or not you will be frequently judged by your appearance. Research carried out in 1981 by Dr A.J. Jouhar and Jean Ann Coraham tested this statement by recording the reactions of personnel officers to CVs sent with photographs of the same women – one set showing them wearing make-up and one of them without. Not only were more of the former offered the jobs but they were offered more money as well.

Looks matter, but this does not mean that you have to go out and spend your last penny on an expensive suit, make-up or hair do; simply that you should avoid extremes of presentation. You can, of course go to an image consultant who, for a fee, will check out your wardrobe and presentation; and there are beauty salons where you can experiment with the products. As a man, you could model yourself on a successful mentor or role model. (Jermyn Street is still reckoned to provide the look for the best dressed men in the world.)

The more attractive you appear to an interviewer the more likely you are to be offered the job. There are some golden rules for interview dressing. Fit the clothes to the job: decide how creative you can be by looking at what others already working there are wearing. Girls can make the mistake of wearing heels too high and skirts too short; men similarly sometimes appear without a tie or with sports-type shoes. Avoid very warm clothes: when you are nervous you will be grateful for lightweight clothing.

Everything you wear should be clean, well-pressed, polished or crisp, depending on the fabric. This helps demonstrate your organized thinking and clean presentation.

Your hair matters too. If you have not been blessed with manageable hair you have a problem because you may be judged to be careless, or even a rebel. Choose a style in which it stays as neat and attractive as possible.

Your insecurities about how you look are fed by the media and all the so-called experts who want you to pay fees to have your image enhanced. In some cases, you are right to feel concerned. A recent US survey of executives showed that 35 per cent of women managers were criticised by their bosses and mentors for a 'poor outward appearance' compared with five per cent of men. The researchers concluded that this was because women were expected to meet more rigorous standards than their male colleagues. Because the boundaries of acceptable dress were very narrow, it was very easy for these women to get it wrong and to be branded as either too dressy or too frumpy.

Personal style and how you fit into your work group will affect your progress more than your competence. How you come across in style and appearance is intangible but important. Some simple principles are:

- Dark suits/outfits are dignified and signify importance
- Light suits/outfits make you more approachable
- Men should never wear patterned socks
- Women should always wear hose
- Good grooming of hair, complextion and clothes matters for everybody
- Leather shoes look good – brogues for men, courts for women

Creating an image

How you present yourself to the world is a form of management. Madison Avenue has led the way in self-image techniques. You can apply them to yourself. It is not simply a question of putting on a front but of letting everyone see the real you – and to remember it.

You are a competent person with valued experience who has achieved a senior position, so say so in the way you speak, walk, sit, dress and communicate. By projecting your status, your credibility will grow and you will be recognized for what you are. Georgette Mossbacher employed her personal publicity agent for two years before it was announced that her husband, Bob, was to be the Secretary of State for Commerce in President Bush's

Administration. She was determined to be recognized in her own right.

You do not have to go as far as she did or get your eyebrows tattooed, but you do want people to pay attention to you. It is a shorthand way of letting them know that you are worth knowing and by dressing in a manner that says so. Quality of cut, fabric, accessories and shoes tell their own story. Designer labels are a current method of saying 'I can afford this', but you do not need to be a stereotype – you can choose your own collection to get your message across.

Men have an apparently more simple task of looking good than women when it comes to clothes. So why do so many still wear cheap shoes and single cuffs, or have pens showing in their top pockets? Yes, they wear suits, shirts and ties, but there are many permutations which can be nearly right or very wrong. A serious businessman is known by the quality of his worsted, his cotton handmade shirt, his silk tie and highly polished leather black shoes, well-trimmed hair and absence of moustache. He does not carry an issue briefcase.

A top businesswoman will have a simple but expertly cut garment with good jewellery, clever, attractive make-up, shining hair, good quality hose and good shoes. She will have a handbag/ file case and will have a well-matched colour scheme.

All will have the appearance of comfort and be able to concentrate on the business in hand rather than on adjusting their clothes. A good clean fragrance rather than a heavy perfume will complete your outfit – whether you are male or female.

So are you well-groomed and do you have a carefully-planned wardrobe? I repeat, it is *quality not quantity* that counts. You breed confidence in your client/banker by wearing clothing and accoutrements which are professionally attractive.

Of course, all clothes look better on a body which is in good condition. You need energy to get, and stay at the top. You need to take care of the only body you have got. In the 1990s, there is a proliferation of gyms, aerobic centres, health farms and suchlike. Take advice from your healthy friends. Regular swimming is known to be the most complete way of exercising, followed by walking regularly at a smart pace for a reasonable distance.

So, you are in good condition, body and clothes; what else do you need to complete your image?

When you are entertained/entertaining, you need to know your way through the restaurant/dining room maze. It is a wise manager who frequents restaurants where good service is guaranteed whenever important guests are included. These days it is accepted that it may be the female who is the host, and restaurants are gradually learning not to guide her to the corner table near the service area.

You should have at least a rudimentary knowledge of the wine list, as well as of the likely menu. When entertaining overseas clients, it is as well to check out their likes and dislikes, or else go somewhere where there is a wide choice. Your reputation as a host matters, so spend time with friends or your partner checking out places first rather than when with your guests.

With corporate entertaining increasing in popularity, you will be invited to, and be reciprocating at, sporting events as much as the city venues. You will enjoy yourself too, if you know your way around the habits and regulations of the racecourse, Henley, Wimbledon, etc, before you go. It is embarrassing to be in the wrong clothes, order the unavailable booze, or miss the turning just because it is a new experience. This is when your networking across many types of people can be very useful, so that you can ensure that you know how to get there and what to do.

Using the media

The Press likes to be able to talk to you and to establish a relationship that is not too friendly and not too remote. Your company will probably have a person or department designated to deal with them, but you should be prepared for those occasions when they approach you.

You cannot win by dispute or argument because journalists have the last word. Not all are as experienced and aware of the details of the situation as you are, so give time and use patience to get the message across. Use fact when possible to back up your statements.

Always be careful about what you choose to reveal to the Press.

Your business strategy will work better the longer no one outside knows about it – you are better advised to keep your secrets than to court the Press so that the world hears about what has been achieved. However, good press attention when you want it for a product or management change, is a different matter. This is the tip of a big iceberg of handling the Press carefully over a long period, so that when you want to feed a story, you will have credibility and they will co-operate.

When you are approached on the telephone for your opinion or for information, listen and ask questions to find out exactly what is being asked for. Then say you will think about it, but be sure to call back within half an hour: this gives you time to collect your thoughts, work out the implications and collate the facts. By phoning back as promised you will gain their confidence.

Also consider other forms of communication. Television is the most powerful and instant way of making an impact on an audience (radio is still widely listened to, but the image with the sound is even stronger). To look and sound natural and convincing is a difficult technique to acquire. Most accomplished TV speakers have undergone careful training; many competent, polished executives crumple before the camera. The use of silence, body language, gestures and personal idiosyncrasies are all exaggerated on the box.

You must find some media projection training if you can, so that you have some insight into how you come across and can remedy the faults and polish your performance. This can also prepare you for difficult interviews; politicians are well trained in the art of deflecting hostile questioning, upstaging the interviewer, rephrasing questions and generally using any advantage they can to get their message of the moment across. You will not be handled with kid gloves once the cameras start rolling, so do not be lulled into false calm beforehand. Be alert, listen and react in a clear, controlled way.

Check what the context of the interview/programme is actually concerned with as opposed to your perception of what it might be. Check who else will be appearing, when and how, as well as your own agenda. If you are not satisfied, it is better to say 'no' rather than to make a fool of yourself.

You will be impressive when you are calm, cool and collected and non-threatening. The more cool you are able to be, the more you will manage to say something which makes sense. When you drop your voice or start mumbling you will be interrupted by the interviewer or co-guest very quickly – and then you will have to wait to return the compliment.

Good performers are able to talk in 40-word stretches, giving the opinion or statement which will provoke a response. You can memorize some suitable phrases for your own situation.

Do not be tempted to stray from your area of expertise, or from what you had prepared to focus on during that session. The interviewer is also a professional and is there to create an entertaining programme, so you could be led down a false line of argument or off your subject if you are not alert.

Always look at the host and let the camera and the cameraman find you and work out the angles. The make-up session before you appear is essential to prevent you from looking like a sweating ghost under the TV lights.

Finally, sit still, do not twitch your limbs, shake your head or clear your throat. Then you will enjoy yourself, so will your audience – and you will stand a chance of getting your message across.

2.6 SUMMARY

Social behaviour affects image as much as dress and stance. Introducing people to each other is another minefield unless you adhere to introducing the 'lesser' to the 'greater'. (You will often have to fall back on your own judgment to work out which is which.) If all else fails, try introducing the friend to the stranger, thus giving the kudos to them.

When travelling, copy the seasoned people who take a minimum of luggage, drink water not alcohol when airborne and have their travel documents and schedule always to hand. The same applies whether you are going to Manchester or Manchuria. Carry your business cards wherever you go. Leave a copy of your schedule at the office and keep in touch.

Your job belongs to your employer – it is a specified function in a corporate matrix. If you don't do it, somebody else will. To reach your goals you must do your job well. But do not get lost in your job: it is not an end in itself, it is a means to an end which is your career.

Your career belongs to you. It is your plan, your dream, your life. You will have many jobs in the course of your career – even if you only have one employer. You will do each one well, but you will be looking beyond each one even as you are doing it. You will be calculating how it can lead you to the next job on the career ladder. You are not just seeking a better job, you are seeking a successful career.

Part II

· 3 ·

Maintaining Your Reputation

In your quest to reach the top, you need to learn as early as possible how to conduct yourself in such a way that every meeting and project with your colleagues leaves them in no doubt about your leadership abilities and eventual entry into senior management. Who better to learn from than people such as your boss and one or several mentors in various parts of the organization? They will be undoubtedly qualified to help you identify the behaviours that constitute success. They can also give you a deeper, more seasoned insight into the workings of the organization so that you can judge how to adjust your behaviour to different social and political nuances. Learn also from those with whom you work – how can you behave in such a way that will engender their respect and motivate them to peform better? This chapter looks at your behaviour from all these different perspectives and explores how you can reassess your behaviour and actions in order to become a more effective person and *perhaps* more likeable! Learning to deal with criticism and using your assertiveness will add to your communication skills. Then you will be able to negotiate well in order to take risks and be aware of opportunites. These are some of the ways to maintain your reputation.

3.1 ROLE MODELS

One of the best and easiest ways of developing your leadership potential is through having an encouraging, involved boss who can act as a positive role model to you. Having such a boss gives you a unique opportunity to observe closely how he or she deals with different situations on a day-to-day basis. You can accelerate your own development through learning not only from your own trial and errors but from your boss's as well. Building such a relationship is well worth the effort – even if it does require considerable time, extra work and dedication to do so.

Don't forget that you have a number of factors on your side – the majority of people are flattered by being asked questions and shown obvious respect (*not* obsequiousness) by a member of their staff. There also, if your organization values training and development, it will reflect well on your boss if he or she is seen to be successfully developing up and coming talent. A word of warning, however. Don't over-do your role. The last thing you want is for your boss to develop a patronizing attitude to you or to begin to think you are slightly helpless or less capable than you really are. Whenever you can, demonstrate to your boss that you are putting into action what you are learning and growing all the time.

Do you have the right boss to learn from? Are you in a job where you can experiment with leadership skills with your own team, division or group? Are you in an organization that is structured in such a way as to nurture and encourage experiment and responsibility at each level? The latter is particularly important; leadership development should be a continuous process. If it is not, you may find that when you are promoted, your organization expects you to change magically overnight into a successful leader. Spare yourself the stress and trauma of such a situation and find an organization that allows you to take more responsibility as and when you are ready.

Ensure that you respect and wish to emulate the leadership style of your boss. National employee surveys reveal that people generally conceive their senior managers as lonely, strong willed, autocratic in style, determinedly ambitious and motivated by money. Respected and effective leaders may well possess these traits but they also need some critical personal skills. In addition to technical competence, the person you choose to emulate should have a style of managing that is full of warmth, enthusiasm and integrity, qualities that successfully motivate a team of people to implement strategy and meet agreed targets. You may be fortunate and recognize that your boss has these qualities and values or you may be in a position where you feel that he or she has qualities which hinder rather than help you in your leadership development. Ask yourself the following questions about your boss to see whether you like or dislike his or her leadership style. When negotiating does your boss:

- Consult you and the other members of your team?
- Implement the 'divide and rule' philosophy?
- Make you all feel that you are being taken for granted?
- Put you in the position of constantly having to work by crisis management rather than working out your objectives together and then carrying them through as planned?
- Sit in an ivory tower and refrain from contributing to the work – is his or her intervention only to comment or criticize spasmodically and unpredictably?
- Communicate well but have difficulty in establishing two way rapport with you?
- Give you an example to follow?

Trouble with a boss is one of the most stressful episodes in working life. When your boss is so outrageously hard to get along with that it is intolerable for all, the stress can reach critical proportions. If this is not to bring your development to an abrupt end, you need strategies for coping – and there *are* advantages in the experience, especially when you win through in the end. All hardships are part of training for success.

When dealing with a manipulative boss you must be aware of how you interact. It is only one step on from learning to say 'no' (which is part of being assertive) to cope with someone who does not or will not share your value system. When that person is your senior, you are in a particularly stressful situation and need all the tips and strategy you can find. You will have suffered from his or her ability to break your defences, to twist your reasoning or to counter your arguments. If this person has learned that they can get what they want regardless of the cost to a relationship or work output, or who prides him/herself on their manipulative skills, then you have to stand your ground. In simple terms, you have to be persistent and say 'no'.

You refrain from becoming loud and aggressive or passive and yielding – you want to get the message across that 'I will not be moved, nor will I fight you'. You have to be repetitive and not deviate from your response of 'no' or your stated demand. It may sound like a broken record to you, but eventually your 'opponent' will hear and realize that you mean what you are saying.

If you have a boss who is constantly asking – albeit with a smile on his or her face – if you will 'just' do this or that, then you have to practise saying 'no' again.

Say 'no I won't' and explain why. If you do this often enough, your boss will get the message that you are not in the business of doing favours for him/her. However, be careful to communicate that it is all right to ask for your abilities and time whenever it is part of corporate or division strategy or your area of responsibility, so that you understand where you each draw the line.

The manipulative boss will usually add either a lollipop or a threat to the request for a favour. In either event, face up to the possibility and state clearly what your role is and why you cannot add on favours. You will need to use your judgment to handle the balancing act between doing your job well and putting it in jeopardy, but, in an organization that values integrity you will shine and progress whenever you show that you are not easily manipulated.

3.2 MENTORS

Mentoring is a two-way process between you and a more experienced person within your company. The term is borrowed from Homer's character Mentor, whom Odysseus assigned to be a friend and advisor to his son Telemachus. By learning from a more experienced person with relevant knowledge and track record, you can accelerate your progress and achieve a higher working profile not just to senior managers in your organization but also in your industry or profession. The mentor gains from being seen to recognize future leaders and if he or she is within your organization, a reputation for grooming successors. Building self-confidence *both* ways is the name of the game. Remember that you can simultaneously have a mentor and act as a mentor to younger fast-track candidates. Also remember that you can have more than one mentor at any given time.

The advantages of learning from a mentor as opposed to your direct boss stem from the fact that you do not formally report to your mentor. This means that he or she is not responsible for appraising your performance and does not have the difficult task of discerning whether and in what way to disclose aspects about your personality and competence which you may have revealed in confidence. In contrast, a mentor is able to guarantee confidentiality. You can afford to reveal your difficulties and confusion to him or her. You can hold safe and open discussions with your mentor about both the personal, professional and organizational connundrums which constantly arise during your climb up the career ladder. The mentor's role is to encourage and promote you further than you can yourself. This form of aid can be particularly valuable if you are impeded by internal politics. Developing a relationship with someone of influence can result in doors suddenly opening within your organization.

You owe it to yourself to fuel your own development by identifying a person or a style you would like to emulate. But don't view a mentoring relationship as your sole vehicle of learning. Keep up to date with papers, magazines and books on subjects related to your corporate life so that you will be better equipped to participate in groups, either within or outside your company. This will be even more effective if you have the benefit of in-house training.

A mentor is a person with whom you should be able to discuss:

• Any choices which have arisen socially, eg, whether to wear suits or dresses to the office, whether to take a partner to an office function, etc

- How to interpret the action and motives of others – did your boss mean to be vindictive when he put blue pen all over your draft report, or was it simply a confirmation of his habit when writing reports himself?
- Motivating your staff – is it worth persevering with someone who is an expert in dumb insolence and incompetent anyway?
- Handling important work events – is doing a presentation in a quiet, clear tone of voice, with a pack of papers for each member, representing the client more appropriate on this occasion than doing the hard sell?
- Promoting yourself – how much time, effort and high profiling should you develop outside the office?
- Handling relationships with peers and senior managers – what strategy you should follow after announcements about internal promotions?
- Handling internal politics – what technique would be most effective at executive board meetings when annual targets are being discussed?

The most imporant thing to know about mentors is what they *cannot* do. A mentor cannot achieve anything if the protegé is not capable of becoming a success on their own. What a mentor can do is help that protegé to know what to do next. He or she can identify career fast tracks in the organization and also highlight the most important skills and experiences that you should be acquiring.

Another important point to remember is that mentoring relationships do and must end eventually. Research shows that mentoring relationships last an average of three or four years. They tend to end for a variety of reasons: a mentor may feel that he or she has given all the help possible and that it is now time for the protegé to stand on his or her own two feet; the protegé may decide to end the relationship because he or she feels the relationship has outlived its usefulness and is in fact now cramping further personal development; or, more simply, promotion may have forced the relationship to end.

As long as you are a good, visible worker, the departure of your mentor should not spell doom or gloom, or the end of all your career hopes. In positive terms, it simply marks a new stage of your development – you might embark on a new mentoring relationship or you might find other methods of development. Whatever you do, you should aim to look for advantages in a seemingly disadvantageous situation. The Chinese have a succinct way of expressing this – their word for 'crisis' is also the word for 'opportunity'. You should expect to feel deflated immediately after being left to fend for yourself.

Keeping these two points in mind, that mentors are not omnipotent and that the relationship must end one day, will help you to be realistic about the benefits of the relationship. *Never* become dependent on your mentor. Learning to roll along and to fit in with any sponsor or mentor is a survival skill, but always stand on your own two feet as well. Hope that you have enough time with a mentor to learn all that there is to know, but always be aware of how you would progress without that protection, and keep in touch with opportunities in general. Learning to live by your mentor's interpretations and guidelines is fine – but even better if you can position yourself to make these deductions for yourself as soon as possible.

Most people average around three to five mentors in the course of a career. You may, of course, have more than one mentor at the same time. This precludes the notion that a mentor is always a boss. It can work well in your favour, for example, when an opportunity arises for a great career move to a competitor, if your mentor/boss depends upon you a good deal, he or she might have a vested interest in advising you to remain where you are – and making it worth your while to do so. Having multiple mentors is also a way of lessening the impact the departure of your main mentor will have on you. Just as teachers can be mentors to students, friends with different experiences can be valuable too. People mentor each other, and a smart person has multiple mentors to call on.

3.3 PROFESSIONAL/PERSONAL TENSIONS

The professional image you project at work is undoubtedly influenced by the way you talk about your life outside the office.

Many people are deeply protective of themselves and hide the pressures and interests which they endure and follow outside office hours. Conversely, some people give blow by blow accounts of their love life, or the latest episode or crisis in the family.

Establishing the right balance between these two extremes is difficult, particularly because the traditional concept of keeping professional and personal life totally separate has gradually been eroded. Nonetheless, there is a dangerous line between appearing as a whole person and as a neurotic one. Talk too much at work and you may well talk yourself out of a job. What you reveal in a state of crisis, or when you are going through a series of upsets, may get thrown back at you at a later stage. You can also put yourself in danger when you reveal the extent of your personal responsibilities. For example, if there is a possibility of a promotion and the choice is between you and someone who has not had to have time off recently, or shown that they were affected by their personal life to the extent of it interfering with their efficiency then they will get the break. It is seen as risky to give it to someone who may repeat a previous performance of unreliability.

Disclosing too much about your personal life can also damage your work relationships. Your bosses and subordinates may enjoy gossip but they will not want to be in daily proximity to someone who may behave erratically or unreasonably because of stress in their personal life.

Disclosing everything about your personal life is a recipe for disaster and contradicts the first rule of relationships according to psychologists. Conversely, creating too much mystery by revealing nothing gives rise to curiosity and unease. It takes effort to filter through just enough information about yourself to show that you are a well-developed personality with a busy life, but this personal censorship is essential to your credibility at work.

Letting people know who you are and what you want increases your accessibility and popularity – so share, but be judicious in what you disclose. Ensure that your company recognizes that, despite your other demands, you are loyal and professional in performing in your job.

The people you can trust at work will probably be few and far between. Your boss, generally speaking, is more interested in getting the job done than in knowing what obstacles you have had to overcome in order to do it. The friends you make may be higher or lower in the company due to common interests (sport, etc) or just plain compatibility, but in the political order of office life, the shifts and ripples of influence change all the time and you may regret a confidence placed with someone who is now in a position to affect you adversely. The general rule is that your private life is devalued by broadcasting it detail by detail.

There can be a gender difference in this difficult balance of your personal and professional life. Women in an attempt to be helpful, often fall into the trap of explaining why they cannot undertake certain tasks, for example, by pointing out that a particular project is due to take place during their children's school holidays, whereas a man is more likely to state casually that he is not available that month.

When a serious problem in your personal life arises, you are more likely to get company sympathy if you have not been 'crying wolf' for months. There is always consideration and compassion for any emergency, catastrophe or upheaval. There is no consideration for you if you are in the habit of wasting time and effort over what others consider as trivial. Growing numbers of companies now have in-house counselling, welfare and other support systems, as it is usually acknowledged that it makes good, cost-effective sense to offer help.

Remember the old adage – once is bad luck, twice is carelessness, but three times is a pattern.

Managing relationships

You will be seen as a reliable professional when you make relationships work well in the office/workplace.

How you are seen includes the perceptions of those who work with and for you. Your clients, guests, competitors, etc, will meet those in your outer office before they meet you. The level of effectiveness, efficiency and receptiveness of these 'first impression' people will be mirroring your style of leadership – and your environmental awareness.

But promoting good relationships and efficiency is only one aspect of managing people. A less obvious aspect is forging friendships and alliances that will help you in your development and performance. Building your image requires help – both personal and professional. It will be impossible to do everything on your own so you need a back-up team for support and as a source of information and advice. This can be a shifting set of people on a totally informal basis.

Your advisers can include any of the following groups:

A. Family, friends, casual social acquaintances
B. Immediate staff; professionals, eg, accountants, lawyers; peers and other workplace colleagues
C. The firm you head or work for: the role models you are following, the eminences, or spiritual advisors, plus the flatterers, and, of course, the mentors
D. Paid professional image makers – public relations consultants, media trainers, lobbyists, etc

You should keep everyone in contact and up to date with your thinking and actions to allow the most beneficial level of contribution possible. There are a few rules, however, for having your staff as advisers:

1. Know your immediate staff and deputies well and have the methods available for motivating them.
2. Get to know your third-tier managers/staff and as many others 'down the line' as possible – they are all in succession and may well be advising you directly one day.
3. A clever way to add to your reputation is to build the reputations of those who work for you. Never look for a member of your staff to be the fall guy or take the blame for you in public, even though you may deal with them in private.

You can also build allies in a more formal way by building a team around you.

In chemistry, power can often be generated by combining a number of unrelated things. The same is true of people – by mixing certain things which do not have much strength on their own, you can create and accomplish more. There are many things that two or more people can do which would not be possible for you to achieve on your own. As the number of people involved increases, so does the available talent, and therefore so does the potential power.

When you work alone, you can succeed only to the extent that you possess all the technical, administrative, managerial and financial capacities required for the work. If you lack one or more of these, your talents will remain under-utilized or wasted. When an organization undertakes any activity, it can use whatever your talents are plus those of others for the additional skills required. In every company at least 20 per cent of the people have untapped abilities which, if properly harnessed, could help it to grow. An organization can maximize human resources when it complements and completes the incomplete inspiration of your inventive mind or the one-sided capacities of the talented person you may be working with. When ideas, systems and skills are combined, new ways emerge to generate a virtually limitless creative power.

Your career requires your commitment. Jobs are ephemeral – your family is not. Your work and your personal life inevitably intertwine – only you can make the balance work. John Harvey-Jones in *Making It Happen* admits that

> *'this involves self-criticism, intellectual honesty of the highest degree about one's own motives and a degree of introspection which most of us find hard to carry out. There cannot be anyone who has held a senior position who is not plagued with continued self-doubt.'*

Top leaders need mental and physical toughness – so do you.

Managing parenthood

The most difficult and important career you will ever have is as a parent. You will be unprepared, unqualified, unappreciated, unsupported and permanently involved. To take on this commitment as well as a full-time career at work, therefore, requires you to be ready, willing and able – even more so if you are female and will be producing the little darlings as well. You will need to get kitted out, acquire skills and increase your competency just as you do in order to become a doctor, lawyer or top manager. You will need the following qualifications:

- Health and strength
- Patience
- Resilience
- Family dynamics
- Counselling – given and taken
- Listening skills
- Networking with other parents
- Ability to eliminate guilt

You will join the throng of inadequate-feeling people when you arrive home with that bundle of joy. You may find yourself plagued by real or imaginary terrors about your child. You will almost certainly find that 24 hours of the day will at first be spent coping, feeding and nurturing your child. All of this may wear down your self-esteem if you don't nurture that too. Do understand that you are the same as everyone else in your fears, but special in your attributes and personality. It is all right to meet the unfamiliar and worry – but remember that you have dealt with similar or worse situations elsewhere and survived.

You will discover that listening with head and heart to what the child is saying is a useful art of engaging each other's attention and thus preventing continuous whingeing. Many parents have managed to give their time at home to the children, their time at work to work – leaving nothing for themselves. If this is you, try to re-jig the balance so that your own needs are given more consideration.

Cutting the apron strings is less traumatic if you have allowed the child to learn and take responsibility gradually and seriously. It is difficult to learn to stand back and let each member of the family take responsibility for their own decisions, but this is the way to solve problems without leaving loose ends; the way in which both parents and children can 'give each other space'.

All you know about bringing up children is based on your own experience at home with your parents/guardians. Are you continuing the same pattern of behaviour? If so, are they applicable today? Lifestyles, expectations and facilities in the 1990s are very different from those of the 1980s, 1970s and 1960s, so exercise your choices and reduce friction by matching life indoors with reality outdoors.

Illness in the family can make inroads on parents' energies and make work almost impossible at times. If you experience the effects of lack of control over your life, lack of recognition for what you are coping with, and even feelings of powerlessness to change the situation, then do look for support and professional help: everyone needs this from time to time to keep career/family/ life in general in perspective.

Being a parent and a worker requires your constant attention. Making both work well can split your commitment so use all the balancing acts you know.

3.4 DEALING WITH CRITICISM

Everybody is sensitive to criticism, so you need to prepare yourself to deal with it. There will always be someone who will criticize you, and sometimes it may be constructive. In order to protect yourself and to be able to recover quickly from being put down or being made to look small, you must learn how to avoid being trapped.

The worst difficulty you can experience is when the other person is trying to shift the blame on to you or away from themselves. They are trying to make themselves appear good or, because they are hurt, insecure or angry, they want to attack you. Your reaction to this will depend on:

- Who the critic is – when the critic is your boss, partner or best friend, you are likely to react strongly and need to protect yourself most because these people are key figures in your life and the outcome could alter the relationship
- Where you are when criticized – being upbraided privately is different from in public, in front of colleagues, in front of

subordinates, or in front of your children
- What the criticism is about – the subject of the criticism may be valid or invalid, trivial or important, old or current, personal or general, and you will react accordingly

The way you react will leave its mark. Negative reactions to feeling hurt, accused, inadequate, in jeopardy, etc, range from passively giving in to argument to being defensive and then being told you are over-emotional or bad-tempered. How can you de-sensitize yourself; stop yourself from being goaded to tears, anger, frustration or humiliation, and be positive in your reaction instead?

A way to react to the critic includes the following three steps:

1. Agreeing with the critic

Usually when you are being criticized, the other person is stating opinions rather than facts. They are expressing, however crudely, the situation as they see it. You may have to work hard to unravel what they are really saying, because critics are often impassioned in making their points. It is important to clarify the situation by using the following statements that seek to minimize conflict and maximize communication:

(A) Yes – I can see why you are saying that, I understand what you are saying
(B) Yes – I would feel exactly the same if it had happened to me

By agreeing, you are avoiding being manipulated. You are not confronting the other person so you are not feeding the aggression. This way you reduce the threatening possibility and make yourself more approachable. You are simply showing that you are receiving – that you are *listening*.

2. Positive criticism

If the criticism is valid, listen and accept it before trying to deal with the situation, and remedy your action where possible. Men and women often differ greatly when criticized. Men frequently cope better; women get upset and fall into the trap of feeling guilty and trying instantly to make good the aspect that has been criticized. Apologize where appropriate, but put the criticism into perspective with the rest of your efforts – remember that you are allowed to make mistakes. But if you are making mistakes often, stop, and deal with the causes. Otherwise continue with your work and learn from the criticism.

The way in which the boss or other person has criticized you will affect your reaction. In the heat of the moment you may be tempted to say something you will regret, in the throes of self-justification. Don't. Keep your cool, even if their criticism is wrong; let the steam go out of the situation before you explain, if you can. Sometimes you will be able to talk it over and even ask what the other person would do in your situation, and so have a joint solution. This may earn you a friend for life.

You may be the butt for someone's anger based on their own insecurity, anxiety or feeling of being threatened. You may take your similar feelings out on someone else. Whichever way it happens, try and stand outside of the situation to find out the real root causes. You will prolong an argument by answering back and it could escalate out of control. When someone is angry with you, give them time to calm down, express their anger and then explain your side of the story simply and without excuse. You may have to apologize and then try and work out a mutually agreed solution. You are allowed to express your feelings but use tactics to diffuse anger rather than inflame it.

Learn to express your annoyance, fury or disappointment for someone's action or lack of it, by being strong, fair and determined not to let it happen again. You will be the strong manager when you sort out the reasons for the problem and avoid repetition. You may need to give support to the person/team for a while, but it is most likely you will gain respect if you do not demonstrate total loss of control. By never getting angry, you will win a reputation for serenity and calmness.

Being described as capable, always able to cope, is usually seen as a compliment. It does, however, place a burden on you to be invincible, strong and competent, and never to complain or cave in. How can you cultivate the inner confidence to be able to cope with this level of expectation?

You can do it by 'judicious assertiveness'. Being assertive and speaking for yourself is to be used cautiously. Used clumsily, assertiveness techniques can simply make you a nuisance to senior managers but when properly used for example by standing up for yourself over a matter that is of serious concern to you they can help to ensure that you are taken seriously by your boss or colleagues. Be consistent about it: simply letting it be known that you know your rights and can act on them if necessary will make other things possible too.

With confidence – and your knowledge of how to be assertive, you will:

- Be able to judge when a request is unreasonable, say no, and offer alternatives
- Be able to give and take criticism face-to-face and know the difference between constructive and destructive innuendo
- Learn to accept a compliment graciously
- Be less in awe of those whom you can see as important
- Be able to talk through disciplinary matters with subordinates
- Be able to judge when to speak at meetings, and deliver clearly and succinctly
- Be able to use humour to defuse angry or potentially insulting remarks
- Learn to discuss openly how you feel without justification or apology
- Be more able to deal with a domineering person and become less domineering yourself
- Be able to cope with strangers, competitive colleagues, rumour-mongers and troublemakers

Assertiveness skills are part of learning to deal with other people at all levels and to harness strong emotions skilfully. These abilities in turn will help you grow your reputation for maturity, strength of character, stamina, flexibility, and gain respect and recognition.

When your critic has stopped talking and you have an

opportunity to take more control, try to direct the discussion into ways of solving the problem. Take one step back, avoid being defensive or aggressive yourself, and you will reduce your sensitivity and thereby enable yourself to be objective.

Agreeing with the criticism may allow the two of you to discover and focus on the *real* cause of complaint, which may not have been your fault at all. If it is your fault, accepting the criticism and using the discussion as a chance to learn will help build a strong and happy relationship. If the criticism is not valid, use the discussion as an opportunity to clear up the misunderstanding.

3. Reflecting the criticism back

This technique follows on from agreement. If the criticism continues and persists, and if your critic is clearly not satisfied with your reaction, it will not be enough simply to try and defuse the situation by agreement. You will need to find out what the real problem is – if only in the mind of your critic.

There is a three-step approach to dealing with these situations:

1. Say 'I'm not sure what you mean. I do not understand exactly what the problem is.' This is a negative enquiry to find out whether your critic has information about you which is wrong or inappropriate.
2. Say 'Will you tell me what is wrong? How is it wrong? When was it wrong? Please give me an example.' Note that you do not ask *why* is it wrong? That may encourage another long diatribe based on opinion. 'Why' may provoke anger.
3. Say 'Is that all or is there more?'

The third step is very important. People often build their complaints up in layers and store up their strongest criticisms until last. That is the point where they have the strongest grievance and the strongest feelings. All the preamble may turn out to be superficial and therefore can be just lightly touched on while you concentrate on the deeper areas. If you avoid getting to this point you will be leaving unfinished business and the possibility of further criticism – and a continuing difficulty in the relationship.

By taking full responsibility for your actions, you are creating the climate for the real problem to be aired. This does not mean that you are saying that the other person's definition of you is true or that you caused the problem, or that you are bad or guilty. Pursue the enquiry until you discover what the dynamics or specifics of the critical statement really are.

After defusing and clarifying the criticism using some of these methods, you can quickly move on and find a solution that will satisfy all parties. Do this by stating a solution and getting agreement or ask your critic to find a solution. If you are offering a solution, be sure to get an approval in response, eg, 'This is what I will do about it. Do you agree?'. If you are asking for a solution, then use direct questions, eg, 'What would you like me to do?' or 'What would help right now?' Phrase your questions in such a way that you will get a reply.

At no time are you getting into an argument, nor have you become defensive or acknowledged that it is your fault, or that what you are being criticized for is bad. You have simply said that it looks like there is a problem, and you are trying to discover what action will help to solve the problem.

Stay calm and keep eye contact throughout the episode. Face your critic and relax. You are trying to discover what this is really all about and you cannot solve the problem until it is clearly defined. Be patient and keep listening and responding positively while probing carefully until you get your answer.

The following checklist may be a useful reminder to you of how to deal with criticism:

- Keep calm, face the critics, look them in the eye
- Agree with their statements
- Find out what they are talking about
- Keep probing until the real problem emerges
- Make them respond to you
- Draw them out by asking, 'Tell me'
- When you have the problem stated, go to the solution
- Get agreement
- Formulate an action plan to finish off the problem

Understanding others' perception of you

There will be times when you are aware that you are under scrutiny or feel uncomfortable with your colleagues. There may be some good reasons for this, such as

- You don't listen to others. Are you preoccupied with your personal life or struggling with your job, or do you just feel that you are more interesting than the others? The outcome is that if you don't show an interest in others they will lose interest in you.
- Are you negative in your responses – looking at the black side of situations or glorying in trouble and problems? Your colleagues will get tired of this attitude and will avoid hearing what you think because they do not want to be depressed. It is easy not to realize how much you demotivate others with this habit.
- Are you the one in the group, office or factory who is always complaining? Nothing is perfect and you will always find something which will annoy you. You can get into this habit when you are finding your work unsatisfactory either because you are under-worked or over-worked. It is acceptable to complain once in a while, when everything is too much or when there is a particular problem which you know can be solved. It is *chronic* complaining that gets you a bad name. It undermines your professionalism and your position. Take stock and find out why you are in this state – it could be a symptom of illness or stress. Deal with it.
- Other people do not like it if you steal their thunder. When someone tells a story, buys new clothes, gets promotion, has a baby, do not plunge in and go one better. Try to give others their space and recognition – this way you will earn yours. Even if all you say is true, you won't come across to others as clever – just as insufferable.
- Losing your temper at the slightest provocation annoys people, especially if they are working with you and it happens frequently. Being constantly dramatic and seeking attention for all you do has the same effect. Even if you are accident

prone or frequently experience dramatic happenings, try to play it down. Gradually you will relax and find it easier to fit in with the group.

- Being over-critical or slow to give praise or to appreciate the efforts put into the job by someone else will bring dislike from equals and fear from subordinates. Constantly finding fault and looking for shortcomings will not endear you to the people with whom you should interact.

- Humour is subjective. There is often one person in the group who prides themselves on cracking jokes, making fun of others and always 'seeing the funny side'. Being the comedy act of the office occasionally lightens the atmosphere; constantly, it is boring. If you fall into this role you will lose the respect you need for co-operation and delegation.

  Being known to lack humour is not respected either. Try to cultivate the ability to smile, to stand aside with detachment and enjoy funny people as well as life's funny moments. The talent for lightening the atmosphere in a tense meeting, office, negotiation with the right phrase, word or attitude is enviable – few of us achieve it often. Being sensitive and compatible with others improves your chances of gaining a balance and establishing mutual liking.

- Are you dependent on your professional life and colleagues for fulfilment in your life? When your personal life is limited or disturbed, you will look for support in your workplace – but by looking to others for help and company and generally leaning on them too much, you will make them fed up with you. You will be isolated for not showing your ability to be independent and live your own life. Making friends at work is a bonus, not a requirement.

- If you demand too much from your colleagues and work-mates, they will resent being told what to do and how to do it your way all the time. Like you, they will want to be appreciated for themselves and to have a two-way relationship. Bossiness is always resented; by showing it you will either create a rebellion or be left alone. You may be right to demand from others, but you need to explain what you want and show that you are not just being autocratic.

- Concentrating solely on your work can easily be misinterpreted by those you work with. Even if you do everything to a high level of perfection, you will not be understood or liked for being so self-contained. People are unnerved by those who don't communicate, mix with them and discuss what is happening in the company. By isolating yourself, even if it is just because you are shy or lack social skills, you will probably end up being disliked.

Think carefully about why some people may not like you. Maybe you try too hard. Maybe you are critical, demanding or gloomy – perhaps for good reasons – but whatever the reasons it will put people off. Not being liked is upsetting and destructive. Here are some remedies:

- Shift the focus from yourself to others
- Listen when people talk to you
- Be open – it's well worth taking the risk
- Use tactfulness to encourage the goodwill of others
- Give compliments when they are due
- Make people laugh, not cry
- Be tolerant and compassionate
- Develop your memory for faces, names and what is said to you
- Look on the bright side as often as possible
- Get others to talk about themselves
- Give colleagues and subordinates the chance to contribute
- Take care of yourself and you will be able to take care of others

3.5 APPLYING ASSERTIVENESS

Assertiveness can be used to accomplish your tasks and to maintain your relationships. It is a way of achieving what you want while holding on to your self-esteem, without feeling humiliated and having to pay for a mistake.

Once you have made your plans, set your goals and have a clear idea of what you wish to accomplish in life, you should attend to the skills you will need to enable you to 'action' your plans and

achieve your objectives. You need to acquire sufficient inter-
personal skills to be effective, and know how to assume a
supervisory management role.

Passive versus aggressive

Unassertiveness shows itself in two extremes of behaviour: passive
or aggressive reactions. Passive behaviour occurs when you feel
inferior to the people you are dealing with. When you give in,
give up, hold back or feel shy you are lacking in self-confidence;
you will end up defeated and perhaps feel humiliated. Aggressive
behaviour is when you try to demonstrate forcefully that you are
superior – when you feel that you know best and are the most
capable. It can cause listeners to react strongly.

Signs of passive behaviour are:

- You are withdrawing – which you show to the other person
  by folding your arms, turning away or pulling back
- You find it difficult to make or hold eye contact and you start
  looking furtive
- Your hands are either tightly clasped or constantly moving
- You find that you are mumbling, or at least speaking in a quiet
  voice

Signs of aggressive behaviour are:

- When you are intense and sit or stand in a rigid position
- You look determined
- You lean forward as if to attack or cast blame
- You put your hands on your hips
- Your face shows anger or disapproval with your eyes holding
  contact in a cold, hard stare, with eyes narrowed
- Your hands start clenching and you start pointing or poking
  with your index finger
- You start lecturing rather than talking and listening
- Your voice becomes hard, sarcastic or even mocking

In contrast, assertive behaviour is when you take charge of a situation yet respect both your own and other's self-esteem and individuality. Signs of assertive behaviour are:

- You face the other person in an open, non-threatening way with arms loosely by your side or in your lap
- You make eye contact comfortably, without staring and by looking at the other person's face
- When you look away, you look back quickly
- When necessary, you gesticulate easily and appropriately
- You keep your voice calm and at an easy pitch so that the hearer can hear without straining
- You have a smile on your face but are not grinning or looking insincere

Being assertive is the way to gain co-operation and keep your self-esteem. If you give in or concede, it is because you want to not because you have been bludgeoned or trapped into doing so. In our culture, most women are conditioned to behave passively to win approbation within the family, with partners and with male bosses. Men are expected to have the opposite role of being aggressive. Both sexes need to modify these patterns of behaviour by improving their sense of identity and self-esteem and becoming more assertive. Fortunately, such a change is gradually beginning to happen.

The basic difference between when you are being assertive and when you are being aggressive is how the receiver reacts. Both kinds of behaviour occur when you are standing up for yourself, but the former will have a positive outcome and the latter will be negative.

Active listening

When you assert your position to another person, you are aiming to communicate, influence and gain respect. When you come across as aggressive, you will have left the other person/s feeling put down, dominated and of little importance.

The first step to being assertive is to learn to listen. Most misunderstandings happen when people don't hear properly, and respond incorrectly. You can practise listening and responding with a friend by listening to them and then repeating back the information so that they can give you the feedback as to how correct you were about what they meant, and vice versa.

Justifiable rights

The second step is to know the rights you are entitled to and to make them part of your thinking. Your rights are:

- To be treated with respect
- To have and express your own feelings and opinions
- To be listened to and taken seriously
- To set your own priorities
- To say 'no' without feeling guilty
- To ask for what you want
- To ask for information from professionals
- To make mistakes
- To choose not to assert yourself

You need to go through these rights, ingest them and put them into your every day life by action, and not by statement. The key to success is to learn to know what you want in any situation, know how you feel or think and state it clearly so that the other person gets the message that you want to convey. This undoes the rule of always being polite, understanding and unselfish, which is what we think it means to say 'I want'. It *can* come across as rude if stated flatly in a demanding tone, but this is not what is meant by 'stating clearly what you want'. It means explaining what your idea is, what you want to get out of the situation, what you are aiming for – in such a way that the other person has heard correctly and can respond to your requirements. When people do *not* know what you want, confusion ensues and confrontation can develop. When *you* are the listener, help the other person to be clear and direct. Both of you should use 'I' when you really mean you are expressing something that you personally think or feel. Not only is it your right to be free to express yourself directly, but it is also important not to confuse matters or deny responsibility by hiding behind phrases such as 'people feel', or 'everyone knows'.

Stating demands

The third step in being assertive is to state what you want or what action you want taken. Avoid hesitating, drawing back or reducing the strength of what you are really trying to get because of the fear of rejection or of the answer being 'no'. Be clear, direct and pleasant. Your choice of words is important. Give the other person a choice – 'I want' should become 'Will you'. This shows that you need an answer, and that you are hoping to get feedback from the listener.

The same step-by-step process will help you to learn to say 'no' without an aftermath of anxiety. Many of us believe that by saying 'no' we are being unco-operative, unhelpful, selfish, and even uncaring. Hearing yourself say 'no' needs to be commonplace so that you are just as familiar with the use of the negative as with the positive, and so ready for when you need to use it. Then you will really be free to choose. Explain why it is not possible for you to accede to the request/demand, but avoid going into minute detail to justify the decision.

It is not just what you say but how you say it that matters. You will be taking a risk in expressing your need or opinion, but you can lessen the risk by knowing how to put it across to gain a positive or co-operative response. You will enjoy the encouraging feedback and successful negotiation which can follow, rather than having to deal with strong, defensive reactions. How you put things across is influenced by your early life, and will depend on how you got your opinions across in the family and at school. You may have to 'unlearn' some behaviour and expressions which are currently second nature to you.

The gender tension is part of your dilemma. Most men expect to be in charge; most women expect to be in supporting roles. Once you realize that being assertive is how you show externally what are you internally and how you are reacting to the other person, then it is easier to grasp. Mutual respect is the ideal – but you have to learn to have respect for others while perhaps having to stand up for yourself at the same time. By asserting your rights without denying others, you will be on the path to success.

Remember that it is often counter-productive to try and attach blame in any situation; it is usually more productive to find out *what* is right rather than *who*.

When you speak clearly, state precisely what you want to say and express your feelings, then you communicate your strength and confidence. It can be extremely difficult to find the right words and not to let words tumble out when you feel aggrieved or very strongly about something so try the following:

a) Take deep breaths first or, if you have time, write down the main points you want to make.

b) Speak slightly slower than usual, look straight at the person and keep your hand movements and gestures under control.

c) Don't shout.

d) Be aware of, and in control of your body language: it will say as much as your words. When you are looking at the other person/s, have firm eye contact rather than staring – and be careful not to point at them.

e) Let your feelings come through one at a time to keep tension from building up.

f) Keep a clear head; inform your listener and explain your stance to them instead of bubbling out a stream of what could be interpreted as abuse.

Being calm and firm makes it possible for listeners to disagree with you without being attacked or judged by you as stupid. They should be allowed to reply to you and explain, so that together you can conclude the discussion satisfactorily. You want to leave them with the impression that you are approachable and perhaps influential – not a monster. This way you cultivate allies, not enemies. Never close a door on someone: you never know when their influence could affect you.

By being unassertive you allow your frustration to build up, filling you with resentment or bitterness. You may suddenly explode at a most unsuitable moment and do yourself – and your career – untold harm. For your own good, learn to say what you are thinking, acquire good timing and use your assertiveness skills. That way, your bosses, colleagues and staff know where they stand and will reciprocate.

Women are often most affected by aggression because they invest a lot in personal relationships and are therefore more affected by upsets. Traditionally, if you are female you will be accustomed to sublimating your needs, and to putting others first. Learning to assert yourself will ensure you don't take this approach too far and become a doormat. Stating your rights shows that you have learnt to value yourself, your skills, your visibility and your position in the company and is true for everybody.

3.6 COMMUNICATION

Conversation is the sum total of verbal signals. How you relate to people varies according to different settings and contexts. The clues you pick up from other people on meeting will depend on whether you have met them before, what you know of them and the circumstances in which you meet. When going to a formal interview or meeting you make sure not to sit too close to others, to listen carefully and to use more formal language than usual. The verbal signals coming across when talking to each other add to the clues through the tone, words, accent and volume.

The sophistication, or otherwise, of grammar, expression and ideas will give you an insight into other people's thinking. Can you read all these signs?

Communication between people is paramount for your career development. In the first instance, it is essential for you to network with useful colleagues. In the company where there is limited communication, however, conversation is seldom easy; getting to know others is difficult, and networking is virtually impossible.

In the second instance, good communication is vital if you are to send accurate messages about yourself to others. Cultivate your sensitivity to what is being said along your networks; check any assumptions which may be made; speak and make statements clearly.

Perhaps most importantly, communication is the key to mobilizing the energy and talent of your staff. Managers and executives are often good at formulating plans and creative strategies, but stumble over the issue of how best to implement them. How do you communicate down the line what needs to be done? How do you come up with practical mechanisms for mobilizing strategic change?

The key is effective communication. Once a strategy is formulated, you will have to take the excitement and understanding of the rewards to people far removed from the formulation meetings. Executives often overlook the internal marketing to their own staff that needs to be done by orientating the planning and strategic thinking towards customers, competitors and distributors in the world outside their companies. But if you are to exploit any marketplace, you will need to act quickly and beat the competitor by running your external and internal marketing programmes at the same time: the goals can be the same for both. You will get the employees' commitment to making the strategy work when you open the channels of communication.

If you are introducing large scale change, employees will usually appreciate being informed (through the unions when relevant) about and involved in such issues as what is being planned and what the values, attitudes and behaviour are which you need to have in place to implement the change. They will also wonder about the consequences of the changes, for example whether other projects will now be scrapped. You can also include shareholders and stakeholders in your internal marketing effort so that they are more ready, willing and able to give their commitment when needed.

(If you are wrestling with the problem of making your professional staff more market-orientated, remember that the example of your own internal marketing programme gives them a model to use themselves.)

When communicating with others, you should try to assess cues like their breathing, facial expression and movement, voice tone, temper and reflection. By listening to both the content and process involved in speaking, you become an active listener, looking for how words and body language match. For example, if you hear someone say quietly 'I am not angry' yet you observe that they are breathing very heavily you will know that their words belie their body language.

Good communication demands that you have clear boundaries, that you take responsibility for your own feelings, perceptions, interpretation and desires. It also means that you do not take responsibility for the other person's feelings, perceptions, interpretations and desires. You should speak in clear language rather than in idiosyncratic innuendo, this way, both sides understand exactly what is wanted.

By communicating as clearly and honestly as you can, you minimize confusion and misunderstanding. By giving feedback you are caring enough to let the other person know what you are really thinking. The basic aids to good communication are:

- A high level of self-awareness and being genuinely interested in others
- A clearly defined understanding of your responsibility and the courage to say 'I'
- The ability to give good feedback about the other's unaware behaviour and your own responses
- A willingness to disclose what you really feel, want and know

The basic aids to dealing with conflict are:

- Being committed to the process of working out differences rather than seeking confrontation. You can learn to strive for understanding and compromise. It is allright to fight, to have problems and disagree, but learn to fight fair if possible – but fight!
- Being assertive and self-valuing, rather than aggressive with others
- Staying in the present, rather than raking up old habits or events
- Avoiding keeping scores and trying to win points
- Talking calmly and discursively, rather than lecturing and pointing the finger
- Sticking to your side of the story rather than ascribing all sorts of meanings and motives to your opposite number

- Being accurate and honest. Do not exaggerate or idealize the situation
- Not arguing about details – agree on the *outcome*
- Not necessarily assigning blame
- Fighting about one issue at a time
- Going for the solution, rather than proving you were right

3.7 NEGOTIATION

Whenever you try to sort out or agree something, you are negotiating. It is not just at the grand level between nations or companies that it is important to understand the art of negotiation – in all the everyday interaction you can forge ahead by reaching satisfactory conclusions on negotiations.

The successful outcome of negotiation is a mutual agreement in which each person included in the discussions has achieved something more than they believe they have given. You may not gain all you wanted, but the aim is to win enough to be satisfied.

Careful planning of negotiations increases your rate of success. You have to assess the position and define your goals for each specific occasion or project. What do you actually want to achieve? What is the minimum you require and will settle for? And what are you prepared to give to get what you want?

You need to try and anticipate what your opposite number will be trying to win from you – and cogitate on what potential tactics might be used and how you will counter them. You should have some alternative solutions and approaches prepared on the basis that nobody will say 'no' to everything.

Having worked out what points you will be trying to make, ensure you have the research and some back-up information ready. The more you know about the situation, the more confident you will feel, and you will be less 'fased' when an unexpected aspect of the negotiation emerges.

Once you have established that you are negotiating with the right person (the one who can make the decision, who has what you want in their control), then you can go ahead. Memorize any statistics or formulae you will need to make your points and be realistic, but do not aim too low: you can always come down from your starting point but can never go up. Keeping your expectations high also helps to bolster your confidence.

The major points to keep in mind when negotiating are:

- You will keep the upper hand more easily when you arrange to meet in territory which is familiar to you
- Wear whatever makes you feel good. The less you are conscious of your appearance or image the more you will be able to concentrate
- You will help yourself by encouraging the other person to start the proceedings. By listening actively you will then be able to calculate your own starting power and gauge the mood
- Do not be afraid to ask – what you do not attempt you will not achieve. No matter how valid your request is, there is no guarantee that you'll get it granted, but *how* you ask could make all the difference to the reaction you receive
- Do not demand – you will come across as threatening, and even if you win the other person will remain defeated and wish to be unobliging
- Do not beg or threaten – this shows your vulnerability
- Keep cool: body language lets either side know how the other is feeling. You should emulate the poker player who is pleasant but gives no signs of what is in his or her hand
- As already discussed being assertive rather than aggressive is more effective. Persuasion is a good way to win, and is much better than intimidating or trying to bully the other person into submission
- Losing your temper loses you control
- You will build up a positive atmosphere by agreeing over items as they arise rather than leaving everything vague for a final denouement
- Don't put all your eggs in one basket. Keep your leverage points by using them economically. Mystery is a good ally – always try to keep your trump card until the last minute
- Practice the art of the possible. You are never going to get everything you would really like, be alert to the maximum which is possible
- Negotiation is not a test of power

- Compromise is not a sign of failure
- When you reach agreement, summarize and record the discussion and make sure that both sides understand clearly what has been determined

3.8 RISKS AND OPPORTUNITIES

On the way to the top you will take risks and your success or failure will determine the speed at which you get there. Risks occur when you cannot guarantee the outcome of an action taken; opportunities occur the same way and provide you with career openings when you grasp them.

You have to be courageous – with a little bit of luck and much perseverence to make it. You get what appear to be breaks to those watching you by taking any chances which appear.

To progress in most organizations you need to be visible to those who can create your opportunities. Hard work is not enough. Somehow you have to be a star in your own right – the risk being that you could make a fool of yourself just as easily as achieve the ratings. It is inevitable that if you seek public recognition (even if it is just in your own small environment) you are exposing yourself, which might affect how someone important to your profession will view you thereafter. You will learn from both success and failure and each gets easier to handle with practice.

When you have spotted a chance to work at a more senior level, or the way to produce something which will create an opportunity for you to be offered more responsibility, you have to assess the risk and then go ahead. These chances do arise from time to time and your antennae need to be out to catch the vibrations and enable you to react positively.

The daily grind will often throw up chances to speak up, to offer to undertake a task, to accept a challenge which will stretch you – and you have no easy way of predicting your ability to see it through. These little steps lead to an increased visibility for you and it is only when you take one after the other that you will find recognition – success is tempered with an element of danger.

Often you will be tempted to keep quiet, to acquiesce and to refrain from suggesting a course of action which you would end up carrying through. This is the lazy reaction, the minimum effort method, the identification of yourself as a co-operative employee rather than a potential boss. Achievers are aware of the rewards of being successful and give themselves reasonably high expectations of achieving them. Low achievement is the result of not being able to visualize being successful and winning the reward – a fear of failure and a low expectancy of winning. Anxiety is caused by uncertainty and fear of failure, but you can lower this anxiety by facing up to challenges, thus discovering either that you have the capabilities to win because it is not as difficult as it appears, or that you can cope with a failure and learn from it. If you don't try out the possibilities you will continue to live with your fear of failure.

The first step in risk taking is to learn how risky it is to play safe. You cannot afford not to take risks. The reward for playing safe is a career of unused opportunities, few people knowing of your existence, and stunted personal growth.

The following checklist provides a simple method of measuring the risk confronting you:

- What is the reward of winning?
- Is it worth the effort?
- What will you learn from the outcome, be it success or failure?
- What is the worst that can happen?
- Can you deal with whatever occurs?
- Is there any preparation you can make to alleviate the risk?
- Are there available alternatives?
- If you do nothing will anything change?

Is this risk a calculated step or a dangerous gamble? Use the process of risk analysis until it becomes habitual. You will discover that it will make a worthwhile contribution to your personal and career growth and give you the courage to live with the inevitable occasional failure. As you practise taking small risks – then bigger and bigger ones as you see the opportunities – your self-confidence will grow. You will be shining and people will notice, including the people who can influence your development.

When you are feeling scared and do not want to go forward, confront it and work out what it is that is frightening you. What really is the worst that can happen? That you lose your job? That you lose money? That you lose friends? That you lose dignity? Often, the very act of confronting these fears reduces them to their correct proportions. Talking to those you know who would understand the situation you are facing, discussing the implications and hearing yourself giving the pros and cons will also help you to bite the bullet.

By developing your judgment when experiencing the results of your choices, you will get more skilled at working out which risks are worth taking and when consciously to hold back. Remember, the biggest risk of all is always the one which catches up with you when you decide to do nothing. So start finding those opportunities now – they are just waiting for you to discover them.

Think through all these facets of your behaviour at work: how you act as a leader; how you speak about your personal life; how you motivate and communicate to your staff; whether you are assertive enough, cope with criticism and accept risk. This may demand a great deal of introspection and some painful self honesty, but you must undergo this if you are to be fully in control of yourself as your career progresses.

Remember that your behaviour and effect on others is like a beacon to more senior people in your organization. These aspects of performance are among the most obvious indicators of your potential to reach positions of considerable influence and responsibility, where the actions and behaviours of leaders are always under intense public scrutiny. Accept that you will always be judged on what *you do and what you say, not what you* meant *to do or thought you did.*

· 4 ·

Proving Your Reputation

Each time you reach for a more responsible position, the selection process gets tougher. For both you and the organizations in which you work, the stakes get higher every time you take a step up the career ladder. Your ability to handle new responsibility, your personality traits, your lifestyle, your values, your aspirations – all are vigorously scrutinized by an employer who wants to take as much speculation and uncertainty as possible away from the selection process. Do you know how to handle yourself when you are under the microscope?

If you are to realize your ambitions, now is the time for you to learn how to do justice to yourself in formal selection procedures. Understand the different ways you can be considered for a new position; gain a sophisticated knowledge of how headhunters work; learn to position yourself to maximum advantage so that even if you are *not* accepted for a position you will feel satisfied with the outcome and know that the selectors made their decision equipped with accurate information about your capabilities.

This chapter helps you to become comfortable with the entire process. The first section helps you to recognize the warning signs – both positive and negative – of when the time is ripe for you to move on in your career. It goes on to look at how you can 'break out' and seize new opportunities, either through being headhunted, putting yourself on the fast track in your organization, seeking a new job, and even, at the extreme, using outplacement firms if you have been made redundant. Whatever the way in which you move on, you need to be equipped to deal with the interviewing process. The chapter goes on to examine interviewing in minute detail so that you can be as prepared as possible and so be more able to keep nervousness and uncertainty at bay.

This chapter also looks at how you as a manager must be a competent selector of staff. The last thing you should want to do is to leave a string of poor appointments as you progress through your organization – you may even find your progress is blocked if you make the mistake of recruiting a poor team around you. In order to avoid this, you should tap into all possible sources of advice about selecting staff. Know how to enlist the support of executive search firms and experts specialized in various forms of personality testing methods.

4.1 REVIEWING ASSETS

Current situation

Are you satisfied with the possibilities offered by your organization for progress or promotion? Are you prepared to stay on regardless of the limitation of opportunity? How good is your knowledge of better opportunities in other companies? The market place is changing fast, mobility of staff and management has accelerated during the last decade, but it will slow down as the demographic shortage of skills begins to show. Have you recognized how you need to adjust to fit the ever-changing pattern?

The decision to move jobs is often a difficult one, requiring much consideration and analysis about what you are leaving and what you are seeking. On average, it takes two years to make a job change. You have to realize why you are seeking a different sphere and what your options are. For example, are you tired of routine, familiar colleagues, limited recognition? Have you a crisis in your life? Do you need a change of location, more income, different responsibilities? Do you want to explore new ideas, a new way of working or a new system? Do you want to have more influence on how your organization works?

Having decided your motivation, you can search to find the position which will fulfil your needs. It is useful to prioritize the importance of the needs, and match them accordingly. Your restlessness may have been triggered by a different boss or colleague or by changes in wider circumstances. It may be because an opportunity has arisen, such as the offer of a job. In any event, there are some basic rules for making the decision to move:

- Analyse the causes – what precisely is the unsettling factor?
- Work out the pros and cons for you, of moving, at this stage
- Make an action plan for your new career step
- Research and collate relevant information
- Be aware of opportunities

Moving is a way of energizing your working life. Never being satisfied within any one job does not mean you are discontented or unhappy. It is evidence of being prepared, of always having an eye to the main chance.

Your strategy for going from A to B may not take you in a straight line: it may be necessary to move sideways, whether functionally or corporately, in order to be on the springboard for the next stage, a biochemist may want some line management experience in order to be regarded seriously for a post as general manager. Similarly, you may realize that you have 'gone up the ladder' in one organization and only have management experience from a single culture, however large or international the company or varied the functions you have covered. The higher up you aim, the broader you need to see and the more global you need to think, so it is advisable to develop your career with a fair degree of mobility.

Until the 1980s, boards of directors preferred making 'safe' predictable senior appointments and it was customary to 'grow their own'. Now companies are searching for senior people with 'add-on' experience to bring in. Those with broad functional and organizational experience are becoming highly sought after.

Another drawback of trying to go up the line within one company is that you can easily get blocked. Waiting for dead men's shoes is not the most motivating way for you to proceed or get known. Most executives now stay in one organization for around five years and then move to another organization after they have achieved several promotions. If your ambition is to be chairperson by the time you are 50, then you need to start with a wide basic experience and build on it with a planned, mobile career.

At some point or other, however, you are bound to find yourself blocked, no matter how skilled or lucky you are. These obstacles can come in the following guises.

Present possibilities

Never aim to be truly indispensable. If you do, don't be surprised if you find that your employer will want to keep you there so make sure you are paid well! Keep career goals in mind all the time and work at fulfilling the criteria of the *next* level. Groom your successor for your present job so that you are free to move up.

This could be your problem if you are in:

- A sale/merger situation
- A declining sector
- A division with a shrinking market share

Major careers can be built up by not giving up in adverse situations and achieving instead a successful turnaround. However, there will be times when it would be wiser to move on. Don't be blinded by misplaced loyalty. Discover what your real situation is and then act.

If you are working for a boss who is not due for a promotion, or who could be promoted before you are ready to take on your boss's level of responsibility, you may have to make a career move elsewhere. Similarly, it might be advisable to make a move if you have a poor relationship with your boss and he or she feels you are unpromotable, or if your boss has a poor reputation in the organization and you find yourself tarred with the same brush.

If your peers are being promoted before you, you need to distinguish whether this is because they are better than you, or whether you are simply not promoting yourself enough. Do not gloss over these occurrences or rationalize them away. Find out why you have been passed over. Consult various corporate tom toms, such as a mentor, colleague or someone else with organizational savvy. If you have enough courage, make a direct approach to your boss.

Decision for change

Do you recognize any of the following danger signs that indicate your career is lying in the doldrums?

1. Younger managers are getting promoted. This is bad news if it means you are not good enough to progress further. Note it quickly and think about moving.
2. It would not be convenient for the company for you to be promoted so groom your replacement and keep superiors posted about his or her progress and your own aspirations.
3. You are perceived to be too old. Are you described as a veteran or one of the old guard in your organization? Reconcile yourself to this situation or get out.
4. Your image is wrong, eg you seem to wear the wrong suits, too long hair, and work too few hours – this indicates that you have failed to understand the corporate culture. Adjust or change your job now.
5. Your organization has brought in someone with new ideas. Where are yours? Why have you not exhibited your innovative notions?
6. Your skills are ignored. You are well qualified but no one is aware of your talent and your desire for promotion. You are obviously not packaging yourself effectively and you are not sufficiently visible. Remember, good work is only half of what is required to move up. Your boss and boss's boss must know you are doing good work.

Don't panic
A hasty job change is likely to be a bad job change: The successful executive changes employment carefully.

4.2 BEING IDENTIFIED

How to be found

When a company or an organization considers that there is a senior position to be filled they will either have someone in mind for promotion or will have to arrange a method of finding a suitable person from elsewhere. This could be through advertising, word of mouth or by using executive search.

The latter method has proved to be a successful way of finding the best person for the post and is being used more and more. Should this be the decision, then the executive search consultant (headhunter) will be appointed and the job description agreed. After briefing meetings with the organization the search begins.

How will you be found?
You will be known for your competency, for doing your job well and to have further potential. Therefore when the researchers begin checking the companies within which the right people for the job may be present, you will be identified.

When the headhunter starts talking to sources – those people in academic institutions, in industry, business and commerce and in associations and other personal networks – who would be likely to know people who would meet the criteria of the post, then your name should come up for discussion. It is preferable that this should happen several times from different sources. Therefore you need to be known about in various places eg universities, City, golf clubs, real time groups, etc. Then you will have a reasonable chance of 'getting into the frame' for consideration as a candidate.

Keep your message simple and memorable so that others can make the connection between your capabilities and the needs of the job which may come up in conversation. Focus carefully on who you want to know your intentions as well as your attributes – then get the word out.

Be active in professional associations, volunteer for committees and any other related extra-company activities. Not only will you gain experience and contacts, you may even meet a headhunter.

You can also get valuable exposure from lecturing, teaching or speaking at meetings. You may be highly qualified and terrific, but only when you let people know – or display your talents – will you benefit.

When a headhunter phones you, either as a source or as a potential candidate, be helpful – suggesting names of suitable candidates, even if they do not want to move, gets them known. Make sure your colleagues/bosses will do the same for you.

To help focus on your headline, ask yourself some basic questions: Do I want to switch jobs now or next year? Is it time to move from a large corporate environment to a smaller entrepreneurial company or do I just want to be in a position to hear about interesting possibilities in my field?

When you decide on your headline, never assume that your job title alone will suffice. Titles are usually long, unmemorable, unwieldy and rarely reveal much about the real responsibilities which you undertake eg, translating the title Senior Vice President, Professional Services Division, International Corporation into 'I am the senior director in charge of finding lawyers for UK companies with overseas connections' will be more meaningful to the listener and is more likely to trigger the mention of your name when someone is looking for a similar designation.

Such headings make what you do vivid and specific. For example, a communications specialist found that her official job description didn't satisfactorily communicate what she did, so the headline she developed was: 'I help people to get their message across'.

When formulating your heading, remember that simplicity is key, because most people can only keep about three pieces of information in their head about someone before their attention span goes and their eyes glaze over. So be specific and give maximum information in the minimum number of words, eg, 'I'm the person who deals with information technology development throughout the western division'.

When you know you want to move on, your concern should include the

activities you are seeking rather than what you will be leaving behind.
When asked, What do you do?, try and avoid giving a chronological outline of your career or describing your job according to how
you spend the majority of your time at work. Both ways will be
unexciting and you will be offered more of the same. Even if you
like what you are doing at present, you should be precise in order
to make yourself memorable. Avoid the statement of your label
only, eg, 'I'm Chief Executive of R.U.S.E'. Instead, explain that
you are in charge of the research, usefulness, selection and
enterprise exercise in your company. It is even better if you can
compare yourself to a well-known figure: 'I am the Bob Reid of
the wire-pulling industry'.

Another way of implanting yourself in someone's memory is to
record a dramatic feat or undertaking for which you were
responsible, eg, 'Last year, I forecast the currency restrictions so
we were well prepared'.

Think about the company, groups and individuals you want to
approach. If you are intending to stay in your field, then your
contacts are your associates, but if you are contemplating a switch
into another area or field of operation, you need to find the
people in the new area rather than expecting old contacts to
facilitate your move. You will be wasting valuable time pressing
your cause in financial services when you want to move into
communications.

The support and networking of a related association group is
useful to speed up the process of finding out about the next area
– as well as providing a practice ground to ensure that what you
think you want is what the job is really all about. Unpaid work as
a volunteer often gives a vital insight into a job. Pick the activities
you know you are good at, eg, telephoning, but make sure you
do the hard parts too, such as cold calls. Use your voluntary life
to display your talents to a wider audience.

To find the job you want, you have got to take the initiative or
react to the advertisement/opening. You could just sit and wait
for someone to call, but having contacts and telling selected
people what you are looking for is far more likely to result in
something positive. Staying in touch and being active both
formally and informally will pay off for you in friendship,

opportunity and a new career decision.

Being blocked is not the same thing as being fired. Most people who are blocked, even blocked permanently, are never fired. So take your time; think about your career goals; seek a job that will move you towards where you want to be, not one that will merely move you out of a bad situation.

In every successful career, there is at least one turning point – a moment when opportunity presents itself. The alert and ambitious executive watches for this moment, and seizes it. It is the chance to break out from the pack of your peers. With proper planning, you can even leapfrog some levels.

The easiest way to break out is never to have to, because you are already ahead of the pack. If you are on the fast track, you are already realizing your potential at all stages in your career development: you simply set yourself the task of succeeding earlier than most people.

Success is a habit that it pays to develop when young. The sooner you *appear* to be successful, the sooner you will be. Set out to be a superstar as early as possible: your efforts and talents will be noticed at school, college and work, as will hard work, determination and being in the right place at the right time. By getting ahead early, you can allow yourself to proceed at a normal pace thereafter.

Getting 'into the frame'

Another way of breaking out is to be headhunted. You can attract the attention of headhunters in the same way you attract the attention of potential employers or, for that matter, your boss's boss – by making yourself visible.

Only about 20 per cent of top jobs are advertised, because companies are using executive search more and more. You must make yourself visible so that when a suitable position becomes available you will be mentioned to the searcher as a person who would be good for the job.

The research departments of search firms read and clip financial papers: do something to get yourself mentioned, and you will end up on major headhunters' files. Search people are good people to make friends with. Even if you are at an early stage of your career, this contact could lead to you being considered for a great opportunity later on.

Send your CV to several executive search companies. Every CV is looked at by research departments, where most are put on file. The best ones are circulated, in summary, to search partners and associates, and filed in the computer system. There they are coded by industry, type of job and position. Search firms are coming to rely more and more on their computerized data bases, so getting into those systems is a very important step.

If you earn more than £30,000 you can phone a leading search firm or two. Ask who specializes in your industry and leave a message with the secretary that you are sending your CV. You will then be allocated directly to a senior consultant, rather than to a junior researcher. On your CV, do not forget to state your current salary/remuneration package. In your covering letter, indicate the kind of job you are interested in, and whether you are willing to move to a different kind of company. When your CV is received, you may get just a thank you note in return. If your accomplishments are sufficiently impressive, you may be invited to a 'get-acquainted' meeting, even though the search firm has nothing for you at the moment. Either way, they'll know you, and that can never hurt. The directory of executive search firms is called *The Executive Grapevine*. So do check the company and the consultant with whom you have arranged a meeting.

One day, either through your efforts to gain attention or because your accomplishments have spoken for themselves, or simply because you happen to be in the right kind of company, a headhunter might telephone and say, 'We are looking for someone to fill such and such a position'. Receiving such a phone call should make you feel good. It is a compliment on what you have already achieved. But before you say yes or no, or anything at all, get up and close your office door. If your office has no door, tell your caller you will get back to him/her. Conversations with headhunters should be conducted in private: an inadvertently eavesdropping boss may be offended or worse to discover you are talking to a headhunter, even if you are about to say 'no thanks'.

Once in private, listen carefully to what is being said. There is no need to be secretive, especially if there is no challenge where you are now, so go and meet with the headhunter – you have nothing to lose.

There is kudos in being headhunted. It is both flattering and disturbing to receive the unexpected phone call from a headhunter: you suddenly feel that someone somewhere has been watching your progress and thinks that your efforts are worthwhile. You have reached the heady heights of having a career opportunity presented to you at the same time as acquiring a new social status.

Before Big Bang this 'body-snatching' only occurred at the highest corporate levels. When the financial services boom brought an insatiable demand for competent people, companies had to use the services of headhunters because they could no longer depend on recruiting successfully through advertising.

Since then headhunting has grown and extended to professional and managerial appointments. The demand for effective senior people is increasing while the supply is reducing due to demographic changes and the requirements for new skills – both of which are forecast to continue. Many companies now look eagerly for executives who have planned their career carefully and who have experience of different functions and companies. These individuals are hard to find, so companies are depending more and more on regular appraisals by external consultants in the race to maximize their human resources. This gives the headhunters the headache of being able to produce good quality candidates quickly when given assignments.

It is no longer just the City and the private sector which are using executive search firms. During the years 1988–1990 I have been involved in finding directors of education for the newly organized Education Authorities, chief executives for national professional organizations and senior officers for forward-looking local authorities – of all political colours. The Civil Service and Utilities as well as the Development Corporations have had cause to look beyond their usual pool of candidates.

So how do the headhunters find you? The days are gone when reliability and loyalty were considered essential qualities for a manager: the experience of different environments is now regarded as essential in order for you to be able to cope with today's global opportunities. You are also expected to have the ability to influence and to have shown that you are able to adapt as circumstances change.

My old boss, Stephen Rowlinson of Korn/Ferry International, used to say, 'people who want to be regarded as shakers and movers have to switch functions as well as jobs'. We look for people who have had job mobility within and between companies and have shown that they are aiming to reach the top by the age of 40. This is different from job-hoppers or, as the Americans call them, wave-skippers and bouncers, those of you who move from job to job before showing your prowess. There have to be signs of *career progression* when you move.

A well-planned career will not make you a specialist at a young age, but will provide you with experience of different roles. The ideal top executive is described as having graduated, spent some time with a blue-chip company, had responsibility within a smaller company, and preferably crossed between public and private sector at some point. You will have differentiated between 'good' companies/sectors and others. You will have accepted working abroad only if you have language skills, and you will only have done an MBA if sponsored by your company.

There is an assumption that if you are being headhunted, you are well-paid. Preoccupation with financial rewards is not a good criterion in your career planning – and grubbing over the details when offered a job is definitely taboo.

You will be well-advised to include the search for power and influence when planning your career. Look at your lesser strengths and work on them using company programmes if relevant and available, but go elsewhere for help if you need to. Going to seminars and conferences helps you to be visible – allowing you to both learn and market yourself at the same time!

The flurry of privatization programmes and takeover activity had a 'hire and fire' beginning but there is now more reappraisal of in-house skills being included. Consultants are brought in to do the management audit, and search is instituted for the very specific gaps identified, covering management for the changes which are inevitable in these situations. So if you are headhunted for a company which has been involved recently in a merger/ takeover, these ruminations may have already taken place, and you have been targeted within their new thinking. Make sure you know what that thinking is because this is the time when last year's annual report or other company information may be well and truly out of date. You may be walking into a still unsettled group of top management. On the other hand, the company may have cited career development and training as top priorities.

Self-appraisal is as important as company knowledge to your progress. You need to be doing this continuously so that you are not mismatched to the real tasks of a job you are offered. You have to depend on the client having briefed the consultant well, and on the consultant being aware of both their needs and yours in order to avoid management blunders and to match you well. At the end of the day, however, the outcome of the headhunter's phone call will depend largely on your competence, capability and commitment.

The power of the jobseeker

The 1990s are predicted to see the traditional power relationship between employer and the job applicant overturned: individuals will be selecting employers and can now take much greater control of the selection process. Peter Heriot, occupational psychologist at Birkbeck College London, points out that if you, as the applicant, are unhappy with the selection process of a company you may well choose to look elsewhere. He predicts that applicants will have much greater power to ask employers probing questions about the vacancy and organization. Take advantage of this shift in power. Demand a full objective set of details about what you are being offered. Looking for a way to develop a relationship with the possible employer rather than being treated as an object at arm's length. Aim for two-way communication and negotiation so that you will be able to perform effectively within the organization.

The way to bring this about is for both sides to describe what the expectations of the job really are so that there is no misunderstanding. You will need to get a detailed job description, including items such as what people who have recently joined the company think about it; and by arranging that you shadow someone for a period of time in order to find out how the culture really works, or at least to be given the opportunity to visit the premises to observe the operation. Sainsburys has been encouraging its graduate trainees to do this for some time, and the Royal Navy has inaugurated a 'job knowledge inventory' which can be copied by other employers. This is a method of questionnaire on a true/false basis about the nature of the vacancy and the range of skills it requires. This can help you and an employer to cut through preconceptions and to build an accurate and detailed picture of the position – minimizing unrealistic expectations on both sides.

Don't let yourself be dazzled by financial incentives. Paul Ormerod, director of economics research at the Henley Centre for Forecasting, is concerned about the use of pay packages as lollipops to get good people. These are being used with young graduates as 'golden hellos' to get them to choose one company rather than another. Whatever stage you are at, you may be tempted to join company 'A' because they are offering more money than company 'B'. Ultimately, you may regret the choice if it does not also offer job satisfaction and career development.

The call for information

When headhunters are looking for people to interview for a job they base their judgments on a number of considerations above and beyond the hard-core statistics of job skills, experience, education and knowledge of an industry. They will be delving into your successes and failures, your capacity for leadership, team play and independent action as well as your creative and intuitive skills; your energy level and the psychological factors that drive you to excel and compete and with your ability to get along with people. They may also explore the quality of your family life and try and find out if you have any addictions which may prevent you from performing to your full potential. Are you prepared for this?

Executive search consultants first meet you through your

resumé, so if yours does not impress they will not call. The information they need should be there, so make sure that you are aware of the information they are seeking. Particularly stress the following aspects of your track record:

- The companies for whom you have worked; describe the character and size of the company (for each job the responsibility you had, the budgetary, strategic and ranking levels)
- Proved profit and loss track record
- Experience in a turnaround situation with a product or decision
- Successful new product introduction or new market development
- Some experience in corporate finance
- A record of developing promising executives
- The level of responsibility both as a professional and as a line manager and the number of people reporting to you
- The successes for which you were directly responsible

Clive & Stokes International, like some other executive search firms, has in-house researchers. We are committed to the use of research, backed by advanced systems informing and supporting the consultants when they are looking for people who will match the criteria of the job specification agreed with the client.

Therefore, your CV should have your career progression, your place in the company structure and your contribution to the bottom line carefully analysed. Then the researchers will identify *you* more easily.

4.3 MEETING THE HEADHUNTER

How search works

Executive search firms place great store in establishing a close working relationship with their clients. As soon as the search begins, the search firm becomes in effect an extension of the client's office. It is essential for the headhunter to know of any development which might impinge upon their assignment, such as changes in job or person specification, personnel changes within the group and public announcements on business or financial matters.

Headhunters usually require that their client does not advertise or use any other recruitment firm while they are working on the assignment. This is because several approaches to the market place can cause confusion which is not in the interest of the client. Moreover, headhunters expect their client to refer to them any candidates who have presented themselves spontaneously to the client; this is to enable the headhunter to consider and compare these candidates with the others.

Most of the executives recommended by headhunters are currently employed, so client companies are expected to respect this fact by minimizing exposure of candidates during the search and interviewing process. This means that no candidate names should be mentioned to anyone other than those executives directly involved in the search effort. Confidential presentation material should not be copied and/or circulated by the client. Most executive search firms look to maintain the highest ethical standards in their work.

Operating procedures
To provide for continuity and good communications, every search at Clive & Stokes International is conducted by two consultants, one of whom will take primary responsibility, together with a research associate. A thorough search throughout identified industries and companies is carried out, as well as presenting candidates known to the firm. This minimizes the risk of appointment of less qualified candidates which often results when other recruitment processes are used. A search assignment is divided into three stages, which can be adapted to suit each individual client's needs and which normally are in step with the fee billing arrangements.

Stage 1 – position specification, research and progress report
1. At Clive & Stokes International, we have detailed discussions with the client's executives to ensure that we understand all the

background and the requirements for a successful appointment.
2. In addition to our understanding of our client's brief, we submit a candidate specification and highlight relevant organizations where suitable candidates might be found.
3. Our research operation includes a systematic and thorough review of target organizations. This review involves a search of our own extensive computer file, the use of external business information services and contact with knowledgeable executives in all areas including those overseas where appropriate.
4. On completion of the research activity, a progress report will be submitted and the client is invited to comment on the coverage of target organizations, qualified candidates, etc. At this stage, profiles of potential candidates will be discussed.

Stage 2 – attracting potential qualified candidates
1. Informal reference checks are made to validate the suitability of potential candidates identified by the research phase.
2. We arrange to meet the candidates in order to arouse their interest in the appointment and to evaluate them against the standards set during our briefing.
3. We select the best candidates for presentation to the client and ensure that they are attracted to the opportunity.
4. We present a confidential written report on each shortlisted candidate, giving personal details, career history, performance at all stages and an appraisal of the candidate relative to the specification.

Stage 3 – securing a successful appointment
1. We arrange meetings between our client and candidates.
2. As well as counselling, we ensure a close involvement with the preferred candidate to resolve any of his or her reservations, to maintain his or her commitment and to achieve a satisfactory conclusion.
3. To ensure the successful resolution of any contentious issue, we assist with the negotiation of mutually acceptable terms prior to these being presented as a formal written offer.
4. We will undertake formal reference checks after the offer has been made, at personal meetings with referees where possible,

subsequently maintaining contact with both client and candidate to ensure that the appointment is successful.

Programme of work

Typically we expect each of the stages to take about one month. Unless the search is on an international scale, we normally expect to submit a formal progress report at the end of four weeks and to provide details of shortlisted candidates some six to eight weeks after commencing the search.

We emphasize that a close reporting relationship will be established, and a client can expect a status report, either written or verbal, on our activities at least every two weeks. Through progress reports, the client obtains a complete insight into our activities and the search becomes an interactive process.

Standard terms

Fee structures will, of course, vary between executive search firms. At Clive & Stokes', for example, our normal charge for our services is one-third of the total expected first year's cash remuneration, with a minimum fee of £18,000 for each executive.

Should the search not be completed during the time over which our retainer is billed, we will continue to work, charging only for the out of pocket expenses. In the event that a solution is not at hand after six months, we have found it mutually desirable to re-evaluate the entire project.

Initial interview

When being interviewed for senior positions, you must expect to be probed, analysed and scrutinized over your tasks, successes and how you achieved them, as well as failures and why they occurred. You may also be asked what you find difficult about people and how you manage them and yourself in difficult situations.

Some enlightened interviewers may be interested in you as a whole person and ask apparently simple questions such as: 'What do you like doing in your spare time?' in order to discover your interests and enthusiasms. They will not be impressed to hear that you do not have any (spare time) or that you flop in front of the television or take the family shopping. You might be asked to give a clue to your creativity by describing an idea you followed up successfully.

Whether you are a team player or a loner at work will be pertinent in most interviews, so if you have not indicated how you work in your description of your career this will be pursued.

Family life and private habits may be investigated – especially if the potential job involves you representing the company in the community or abroad. You may feel this is an invasion of your privacy but sometimes it is company policy, so be prepared. The headhunter or recruiter may have been instructed by the client that they are seeking full commitment which includes the family, for example. They will have asked sources or sometimes referees early on in the procedure about any known problems such as alcoholism, but drugs are usually dealt with by tests included in the company medical.

There are always some recruiters who believe in provoking candidates into controversial discussion or heated arguments to test their control or spiritedness in such circumstances. Provided you do not try to dominate or to win the argument at any cost, then do enter into the spirit of this game. Your sensitivity and ability to use a blend of diplomacy and strong thinking will be noted.

It is all right to take charge of the interview by asking questions about the company, including the financial condition, style of management, fate of your predecessor, staff mobility and so on. You will be seen as astute provided you are not asking for information which you are already expected to know. There is rarely a right time in an interview to go into the details of the package they are offering you: this should be done with discretion elsewhere, either with the personnel director or through the headhunter at another time.

Often you will not be told the name of the company until the second or third round of interviews, so it would be premature to try and find out too early. However, I do believe that we have reached a point where the mystique of the client is somewhat unnecessary.

All recruiters want you to sell yourself, so always be enthusiastic. You will have some idea of the level of interest in you by the length of time you are given for the interview (45 minutes is OK; one/one-and-a-half hours is better; two hours means it is getting serious).

When asked for references, give the names of referees (after you have asked them) rather than giving general purpose already written documents. You can stipulate when they can be contacted. Otherwise, you are in the hands of the recruiter to a large extent as to who he or she will contact to ask about you. Some stick to your list, others speak to former or current staff colleagues, bosses and clients. You can never be sure what people will actually say when talked to on the telephone by a skilled recruiter. There is nothing you can do about what is said this way and your reputation can be made or broken during these conversations. Your only protection is to keep good relationships at all times, to brief anyone who might be contacted and pray that your track record is going to come through in its complete positive form. When anything is written you do have legal redress, but most people know that and are careful.

When invited for an interview via a search firm, ask for the job description and any other information about the company. Study it and then make up your mind quickly whether you are interested or not. If the job has less opportunity than where you are now, say 'no'. Don't be coy – this is too important for game-playing.

Self-projection

It does not matter (in principle) whether you are preparing to present yourself for interview by one person, a panel, an unknown number, or even in front of a camera. Self-projection or selling yourself is what it is all about. In comfortable circumstances – at home, with colleagues, with clients or with groups of similarly interested people – you may have become used to putting yourself across. It is when you stop and think of putting yourself up for inspection, for judgment, for cross-examination, that the colly-wobbles begin.

Nervousness may catch you out in unexpected ways. It is not the shake in the hand when receiving the proffered cup of coffee which is the only tripping device. You may find your co-ordination in general is out of tune: books, umbrella, handbag, coat, etc, all become weapons of confusion. Try to keep these items to a minimum – wear familiar shoes, comfortable clothes and a handbag/briefcase big enough to find papers easily in.

Do your shopping well in advance, experiment with accessories, combine the colours, work out the image – and mend the tear, sew the button, clean the shoes when you have plenty of time. You will achieve your goal of looking your best by playing with alternatives when you are relaxed. Vital necessities to true perception of yourself are good light and good full-length mirrors. Be truthful, be wide-awake, be careful when assessing yourself and check all angles.

It almost goes without saying that the interviewer's first impression of you is very important. Whether you like it or not, many decisions are based on first reactions when you meet someone. This should not be the case, as directors or interviewers at any level should have had training, or at least a level of awareness, to prevent this instant assessment. However, the first impression still remains as a potent factor in any appointment discussions. Check your presentation *now*, and be careful to avoid the following major presentation faults:

1. The irresolute look – showing how unsure you are of where you are and what you are expecting, and evading eye-to-eye contact.
2. Fiddling, eg, with hands – turn the twitch or nervous movement into a positive gesture to demonstrate what you are saying positively but with style.
3. Sitting – it is easier to concentrate on the matter in hand while seated at a table. The open 'informal' arrangement of seats causes the 'open fly' or 'ladder in the stocking' uncomfortable thinking. However, it is a general rule that sitting four-square in whatever chair is provided, upright and looking directly ahead is easiest to

manage. You need rehearsal for this too – so that you appear relaxed and non-aggressive; keen but not over-eager.

4. Gabbling – take deep breaths before, during and after entering the interview room. Walk steadily to your place and take your time to sit down. Then look up, clearly waiting to be spoken to. Pace your words in reply; take time to consider rather than rushing; wait for the full question, and maybe follow-up ones too.

Many women have problems of low self-esteem, with the result that they do not plan their careers and go from job to job rather than promotion to promotion. They often betray this attitude when they come to interviews by focusing on short-term considerations. Men in contrast, tend to have an eye on the long-term career prospects. When interviewing women, I find it harder to keep them concentrated on their professional experiences than the men: it is unusual for a man to say that he left a job for family reasons, even when this is the case, instead he will give a more pertinent work-related reason.

The level of expectation by women generally is lower than that of men. Recently, an advert for a job at a reasonably high salary had very few replies from women managers. When circumstances changed and it was re-advertised at a lower salary, many more applied. The Personnel Director was intrigued and made enquiries: the applicants admitted that they knew they were capable of the tasks in the job description but did not believe that they would be considered at the higher salary. This makes it difficult for headhunters to find senior women. They are even better than men at burying themselves in their jobs and not surfacing when suitable posts arise.

So if you are a talented woman, throw all your energy into selling yourself well: mastering this art is essential for career progress. When you see senior jobs advertised relevant to your experience, *apply*. You can make sure that references are not taken up until the appointment stage, so you need not disrupt your existing position. Don't hesitate to apply for jobs paying more than you are earning now; remember that your male counterpart will in all likelihood eagerly apply, even if he does not possess all the qualities required by the vacant position. Do the same – remember that there is a learning curve for anyone in a new post. You will not be expected to deliver perfect performance on day one. Take a risk and apply and let your recruiters decide if you are right for the job.

In any interview you must be yourself: trying to play the part you imagine the interviewer wants to see is a hiding to nothing. Play-acting is easily detected, so the old adage of taking a deep breath then letting go is a good one.

You will, of course, have found out as much as possible about the company, read the last annual report if possible, and talked to anyone you know who is working there. Finding out more precisely about the job is more difficult beforehand, but it is part of the job of the interviewer, especially if he or she is a headhunter, to brief you.

When being taken through your CV, avoid giving a repetitive chronological listing of your jobs: concentrate on why you chose those 'A' Level subjects, what influenced you to choose that degree at that college, or why you chose to go for a particular profession. Explain the *circumstances* of each career move; show how you planned your career and how each step has been leading you nearer your goal. You may have applied for and accepted opportunities, but it will be more impressive to show how you worked out what you needed to fulfil your plan. Then indicate how the new position would continue this process.

During the interview, let the interviewer set the pace and try not to speed up the dialogue. It is always helpful to give examples of what you are referring to and the nature of your responsibility. It is also answering the purpose of the session to give figures, ie budgets or numbers of people reporting to you at particular times so that you give a clear idea of the scope of your responsibilities. If you have always worked in the private sector or a more entrepreneurial environment where it is customary to relate everything to the bottom line (profit made), you will find it more difficult to pull your contribution out from the workings, and to explain your value. In this situation it is helpful to be anecdotal at times – to illustrate what you are describing.

Women often find it hard to balance their natural warmth with detachment in interviews and sometimes over-do the latter, giving the impression that they are aloof. An interviewer needs to like you and be confident of you as an 'all-round' person when putting you forward for a job. You should set out to convince the interviewer that you are open, capable, confident and available to further your career and the company's objectives.

Methods of interviewing

Interviews should be interesting for both the interviewer and for you. Once you are comfortable with each other, feel free to ask questions yourself. Women often assume too much and do not ask probing questions about the job. This is sometimes to do with the relief they feel about having got so far and some disbelief that they will be offered the job, so that they are willing to accept the job with all its wrinkles. Many men assume that they may well be offered the job and are therefore more geared to finding out exactly what it entails and will even try to negotiate more for themselves.

If the interviewer is willing to discuss salary, job title and the authority within the job, then this is your chance to show what you really want and confer. However, this is not always within the brief of the interviewer, so do not persist if you discover that this is not the right person with whom to negotiate.

Most senior posts require more than one interview. Always try and make a good impression, even in the early round, otherwise you may not go further, no matter how well-qualified you are.

Some interviewers revel in asking difficult questions with no obvious answer (e.g. political or collegiate) or make provocative statements to test how you rise to the challenge. Stop and think, then give your considered opinion. There is not a 'right' answer, just the way you answer is probably more what they are investigating. If you find a hostile atmosphere developing, try and disagree pleasantly and with grace, rather than trying to score points. You are not in control here, so extricate yourself as best you can.

When the interviewer says 'Tell me about yourself', or asks another equally vague and open-ended question, you are being tested on your ability to react quickly and think on your feet: this is not an opportunity to give a chronological monologue of your career. The jobs you have done and their sequence are listed in the CV in front of the interviewer. This is your chance to *shine*; to outline several of your strong points and accomplishments, and to explain the projects for which you have had responsibility.

The interviewer may listen carefully and give you the encouraging look or nod from time to time, but do not be put off by lack of comment or silence.

When your work experience is limited, go into detail about your learning powers and the reasons why you wanted to follow this particular career path. You want to display yourself as a whole person with interests and activities outside work. Don't be shy – if you won the tennis tournament, say so. Keep an eye on the interest level of your listener and be careful to sum up the main points and stop talking as soon as appropriate: nothing is more irritating than a repetitive rambling to fill the silence.

Another common opening question is something like, 'Why do you think you are qualified for this job?' Discuss your strongest points first. Start with your academic or professional qualifications and then go on to the experience you have had which most closely relates to the requirements of the job description. You will give a good impression by giving dates, names of bosses/colleagues involved and some figures which give the scope of the concern accurately. Practice saying such things out loud at home, so that you flow and statements sound natural.

Your answer to questions about why you want to work for the company could give you away if you have no idea, or the wrong idea, of what goes on in the organization. Try and procure any literature available from the company's press office or the library before the interview day, and read them carefully, noting any questions triggered. The trade publications will be sources of information when the company is well-known, and local business-people will probably have an opinion to offer. If you have trouble finding out details of the company itself, fall back on a general knowledge of the sector, the industry and its current position in the economy.

When asked why you want to move from your present job, explain positively about why you went there, why you have enjoyed your time there and the good points of the company. This is not the time or place to have a moan about bosses, colleagues, product or management: the interviewer will be hyper-sensitive to the possibility that you are a misfit, disloyal, a trouble-maker or just plain inadequate. Without being obviously insincere, concentrate on the further responsibility, challenge and advancement that you are seeking. Discuss the extra skills you want to learn by joining this company only if you are really sure that the job will offer you the opportunity to develop them.

To the question, 'Where do you want to be in five years time', I once got the frank answer 'in love, in work and in London'. It is better to be realistic than pompous or misunderstood, for example by stating baldly, 'I want to be the Chairman'. Even the interviewer may feel threatened by this sort of determination, so balance it carefully and don't be too vague either. It is safer to dwell upon a positive generalism and let the interviewer follow it up, for example 'I hope that my hard work will gain recognition, that my addition to the team will work well and that we achieve the targets'. Your answer will reveal your understanding of the company promotion system or culture, so think carefully about this question beforehand. Your knowledge of the organization should be augmented by the briefing from the headhunter.

When probed about your weaknesses, admit that you have some. Don't declare that you 'hate getting up in the morning', or that you 'enjoy a pint at lunchtime', for obvious reasons. Relate weaknesses revealed in your previous work, but only when you can show how you developed or solved the problem: have some examples ready – you will make a good impression by showing that you accept blame and remedy situations rather than blaming colleagues or machinery. The same principles apply when discussing your strengths.

4.4 THE SELECTION PROCESS – AS THE CANDIDATE

Making contact

The next stage will be a further interview with the person/s for whom you will be working if the job was advertised, and with the client company if you have been headhunted. Now is your chance to get a feel for the organization. You will be given an introduction, presentation or a 'walkabout'. You can then assess how structured the organization is, how friendly the people are, how prosperous it appears and what standard of performance is apparent. You will also see the product, where relevant. If you are not offered the opportunity to look around, you might ask the original interviewer if this is possible – giving them time to plan your visit.

Where there is a formal procedure, say in the case of the appointment of a chief executive of a City Council, you will be notified when you are shortlisted of the dates and times of meetings. Such procedures can be quite time-consuming and may necessitate more than one night's stay in a hotel. You will be invited to meet council members and sometimes senior officers at an informal meal/reception. This is where mutual assessments are made and your social skills tested.

Following from that will be an interview before a large representative panel, sometimes with observers in attendance. This could be a question and answer session, or could include a case study typewritten report which you are given to do on arrival to present during the interview. After this session, successful final candidates will be asked to return for the appointment interview. In between these dates, you may be asked to attend elsewhere for psychometric testing (see p.130). Every council is different, but you may have to produce a written piece again, as well as answering questions or expanding on earlier discussion. Try not to repeat your previous performance, as you will be facing the same people again who will be looking for what else you have to offer.

Always make sure that if you are offered the job, you are willing and able to accept before attending this final interview. It is regarded as unprofessional to drop out at the last moment and may well militate against your future prospects.

Interview procedure

A good interviewer will always probe into uncertain areas, so think beforehand how to answer the obvious problem question.

Avoid going into massive detail about filing systems or some irrelevant staff conflict unless you really need to illustrate how you changed the whole thing effectively.

It still happens from time to time that you are asked more domestic questions. Do not worry about this if it happens to you. Just show your transferable skills in action and demonstrate how you have managed your life to be able to fully concentrate when in the workplace.

It is relatively easy to check out your role in your present job. Headhunters especially have a wide network within companies, so the chances are high that they can check with a source the real level of your responsibility and the quality of your work. Try and give a realistic assessment of your qualities and do not exaggerate your power base. It adds realism to your description to cover the routine, the methodology, the way you motivate your staff and how you deal with report writing, other paperwork and, above all, how you deal with clients/customers. When you have not changed jobs for some time you need to sit down and list what you actually do because a lot may have become habit. Women who have spent many years managing a home and family have many management skills that they don't recognize as such but which are transferable to the workplace.

When asked about salary or the remuneration package, show that you have studied the terms and conditions offered. The interviewer will assume, since you are sitting there, they are more or less acceptable, but there is always room for negotiation, provided you can prove your case. Think through what the job is *worth* rather than what you need to earn, and always talk of salaries in annual terms.

When there is a big gap between what you are earning now and what is on the table, you need to explain convincingly why you think you should be considered. If what is being offered is a lot more, you may be able to analyse the remuneration practices of your present company in relation to the new one (someone moving from public sector to private sector may find themselves in this dilemma).

Conversely, if what is offered is lower than your present pay, you need to give a good reason for being prepared to take less.

The most valid is to have a particular opportunity or skills training, or to move to a company of note from a company which has had to pay above market rates to get people to stay there.

Many companies will use your present salary to work out their offer – hoping to get away with as little as possible – so be prepared to argue intelligently about how you see the price for the job. Women have this problem frequently because of traditional pay structures which lead to them earning only three quarters the salary of their male counterparts.

You should also take into account the fringe benefits you are leaving or acquiring. In any event, think it through and listen first, before putting a price on yourself.

Talk about money last. One of the games you must learn to play is to act as if salary is not very important to you, even though it probably is. Most job applicants want to start by talking about money. Most employers want to end there. Go along with them. If they decide they want you for the job £5000 more or less isn't going to make much difference to them. You will do yourself a favour by waiting. Don't talk about retirement benefits and vacation until after the job offer. Interviewers want people who are concerned about doing the job, not getting away from it!

Interviews are stressful but keep in mind that you are already ahead by being invited. You have already made a good impression somehow, so you don't have to make a big point of establishing yourself. You don't have to reiterate your CV; you can afford to be a little more relaxed, a little more quiet, a little more thoughtful – all of which will make for a better interview.

Between jobs

If it happens to you, face up to it quickly and act. The best way to find a job is to have one; you will remain demoralized without a job, so try and negotiate with your employer that you stay where you are until you have found something else – then get down to finding a new one at the earliest opportunity.

Do not waste time waiting for a miracle. Do not succumb to shell-shock or moaning. During notice, evaluate your skills and make a list of companies which might use them (include out of town companies as well as local ones).

Don't be afraid to ask what your present company is going to say about you when asked for a reference: it is your right to know and it could make or break your future. Think of everyone who might be contacted to help you in your job-search. Keep in mind you need a job in thirty days, not next year. In every interview, convey the impression without sounding desperate that you are not just browsing in the market – that this is the job you want.

You may be fortunate and find that your company offers you professional support to find a new job. Nowadays, few senior managers are sacked or made redundant, without being offered outplacement counselling by their company in order to aid them in their search for a new job. The main objective of the career consultant in the outplacement agency to which you may find yourself sent is to help you find another job, but if you are wise you will take the opportunity to take stock and assess the direction you wish to take from this point onwards. You will be offered help with self-appraisal and career-appraisal as well as the job search. You will be involved in many sessions with your counsellor and with a psychometric testing consultant, and together you will create the up-to-date profile of you, your ambitions and your abilities.

Whether you use this time as a crutch or as a stimulus for change is up to you. Your reaction will, initially, depend on the way the news was broken to you by the employer, and subsequently by your own attitude and strengths. The older you are the more devastated you may be due to the recent history of difficulty for older people in getting reinstated in the job market. Now, of course, the demand for, and recognition of, the more mature manager is growing.

After breaking the news to your family/colleagues, you can settle down to the process of job hunting. If you have not been in the habit of keeping your CV up to date, now is the time to do it. Search consultants are including people from outplacement consultancies in their lists now as it is more commonplace to find good people in this predicament. The perception that a redundant person is inferior is gradually being accepted as a myth, as the reasons for being without a job become wider and wider to include many *good* reasons.

You will fare better and be recruited quicker when you have above-average interest in computer-based work, production administration or marketing. Until very recently those of you with backgrounds based on financial, legal or secretarial work had limited possibilities, but even this is changing now. With the new focus on nurturing the human resources in a company, it may soon become apparent that those who recruit and those who discharge will be more careful and improve their ability to recognize talent in their managers.

4.5 SELECTION PROCESS – AS THE CLIENT

When you have identified the need to fill a senior post, there are many ways to set about finding a good person capable of doing the job. You may have already 'grown your own' within the company, so that a promotion would solve the problem. This is the most cost-effective and efficient way of growing a senior team. Not so long ago, it was customary at this level to elevate or bring in a relative of the Board member/s, or to spread the word around the 'old boy network'. This has never been a foolproof method and today it is a totally inadequate way of finding people ready to undertake senior responsibilities. You should be aware that there is now a range of professional selection services available. Research into these different approaches and choose the most appropriate for your needs. Gain a reputation for being skilful at making key appointments and for creating balanced, well per-forming teams.

Using executive search

When you want to recruit or search externally, there are several routes with different emphases available to you. Recruitment can be done directly by your company advertising or by using an agency which selects applicants for you from the general response, or from its own books.

However, when you need to find the best person for the job, as opposed to the best person from among those already job hunting, then executive search is most appropriate.

Headhunters are of most value to you when you are seeking scarce or specific skills to enable the person to fulfil the requirements of a post. Headhunters try to find the person with the competence, track record and chemistry which will make the match with the client company work well.

Many senior positions are now filled by this method. The people who are headhunted are now becoming accustomed to being targeted when jobs come up, and no longer check advertisements or consider *applying* for jobs.

Candidates found by headhunters for you will be as outstanding as the parameters of the job, the remuneration and the realistic career development possible, will allow. Executive search is a young profession (20–30 years old) grown out of general management consultancy. The sector is growing at the rate of about 50 start-up companies per year in the UK, so you need to choose the company and people in it who understand your business best.

Search firms generally charge either a minimum fee, for example 30 per cent of the remuneration package offered to the successful candidate (normally about £18,000 per search). Where there has been a wide flung international search, there may be add-on fees. In all cases agreed expenses, VAT and psychometric testing (if required) are extra. For some public sector or national posts advertising as well as a search procedure may be required, and these costs will be extra too.

The majority of assignments take a minimum of 12 weeks and an average of 24, and a few continue until the candidate is found to the satisfaction of you, the client. The reputation of the headhunter is at stake, so the executive search firm (if it is good) will be anxious to complete the assignment well so that you will use it again. In most assignments the arrangement continues until the appointee has completed six months in a post, but the responsibility of the headhunter should only end at that point when both client and candidate are happy. This is a different procedure from that used by recruiting agencies, whose job is complete when the candidate is identified for a job.

There are some useful criteria to check executive search firms against. In order to choose and work with the headhunters for your maximum benefit, bear in mind the following points.

First of all, meet the consultant who will be dealing with you throughout the assignment. Don't assume that the person who comes to do the presentation about the service will do the assignment. Normally, the project is delegated to another (probably more junior) consultant once you have appointed the company to do the search.

The relationship between you and the consultant is key to the success of the outcome of the search. That consultant will be the public relations officer and mouthpiece for your company when discussing the project with sources and candidates, so your mutual understanding is vital.

The consultant will need to meet people at different levels in your company who will be colleagues of, or who will report to the person who is being sought. So long as you know your organization and prepare your brief well, then a relevant, pertinent and effective job description can be evolved and implemented: you will be able to explain the relationship and the flaws with which the person will have to contend on arrival. The consultant should then respond with an understanding of what has been gathered about the role and the person's profile, so that all are working on the same wavelength. The more that is communicated during the early stages, the more quickly the process will be executed.

Where the executive search company deals with the private sector, it will be difficult for you to have access to their confidential/client lists so that you can assess their past performance. Nevertheless, you should talk to other companies and find out what they thought of the search company.

In certain cases, you must determine that the consultant not only has a working knowledge of your sector, but also of the specialisms involved in the post. The majority of executive search firms do have certain expertise, so check that they deal with it, or with whatever it is that you need.

Behind each good consultant there is an even better researcher who, along with a database, will seek out the vital information so that the search probes into each nook and cranny to find the right people. If you can, try to meet the researcher so that you can give him or her a better feel for the search. At Clive & Stokes International we have four in-house senior researchers for six/eight consultants.

You should be kept in constant contact with the consultant so that you will be made aware of progress and of any problem areas which have arisen – this could be anything from salary competitiveness to relocation needs or public perception of your company.

You must allow the headhunter time to carry out a really thorough search; to follow every trail and clue. You should expect to have sight of shortlisted candidate lists somewhere between four and eight weeks after the search has commenced. Setting up the timetable from day one is helpful to all concerned, provided realistic dates are agreed. You cannot rush this process.

The interview procedure is normally individually tailored to your company. Whether it will be you on your own meeting the candidates, or the Board, or a selection panel, etc, will affect the length of time involved in the sessions. It is being understood more and more that candidates should be able to have some impression of the organization before the interview. This has been more commonplace in public sector than private – where members and officers have invited prospective people to meet with them informally, often the evening before. The headhunter needs to be able to brief the candidates thoroughly. It is important to have two executive consultants present at all meetings in order to provide advice to you and give feedback to candidates efficiently and effectively.

As the client, you have the last word and control over the procedure, but the consultant may be able to advise about new methods which have been successful, such as the use of written tests. Depending on the nature of the post, the interviews can then be thought through so that the candidate can expose the strengths and weaknesses which closely relate to the job. The momentum of the process needs to be maintained for both yourself and the candidate, so knowing the timetable does help.

It is useful for you to check whether any likely internal candidates equate with the standards of the external – the consultant should suggest this to you. Each candidate meeting the criteria of the job should udergo the same process. This may include some or all of the internal candidates. By doing this, you and your organization will not be accused of overlooking existing staff and you will also be sure that you have the best candidate for the job.

Fees should be established in advance of the search commencing, with you and the consultant having a clear understanding of amounts, dates due, and final payments.

You should be aware of any conflicts of interest from your company standpoint; tell the consultant where not to go to 'tell the story'. Conversely, check that the consultant has not got an 'off-limits' agreement with the main companies from which you know you could find people relevant to your company needs. Executive search companies usually agree not to go to any client company and talk to any person about other jobs for up to two years after a placement, in order to safeguard confidentiality and to prevent the use of privileged knowledge of the skills base to further the interest of probable competitors.

Finally, don't waste all this time and investment by avoiding appointing someone who is smarter than you. Many managers give in to their fears of being upstaged and select candidates who they feel they can safely control. When you follow this practice you end up with people lacking initiative, who are limited when you try to delegate and who cause frustration to all.

Be strong – find the very best people available to do the job; people with the potential to grow. Then you will be stretched too; you will be leading first-rate people and you will be the example they will follow. The company will thrive and grow with this amount of stimulation. Says David Ogilvy of Ogilvy & Mather, 'When you use people smaller than you, there will be a company of dwarfs: when you hire people bigger than you, you will have a company of giants'.

You should hire people to give your company depth of experience and look for people with particular expertise to meet specific needs. You can avoid the obvious candidate from within the same industry sector by probing into what is being brought to your company and by making sure that that is really what you want. You will be looking also for the person with innovative ideas

to inspire your existing staff, but you must be sure that they will
carry these ideas through.

Psychometric testing

Attitudes to psychometric testing have changed greatly since the
negative response when Sir Michael Edwardes, on his arrival as
Chairman at Dunlop, immediately had management teams tested:
they did not understand the relevance of the tests to their jobs
and felt insulted. Today, nearly all mobile senior managers expect
the psychometric test to be part of the selection process, just as
they expect to be headhunted candidates for a post and not
applications in response to an advert.

Despite the widespread use of psychometric testing, many
candidates I have booked for a day of tests are apprehensive at
least, terrified at worst when they arrive on the day, regardless of
how much the procedure has been explained. When they have
survived, they are delighted to have been through the experience
and they look forward to the debriefing and feedback. When
appointed, these senior managers who have been tested often go
on to use the tests when they are going through selection and
recruitment procedures for staff themselves.

The main uses for psychometric testing are:

• As an extra tool in the selection process. Outside screening by
  psychologists is often regarded as superior to the more
  subjective interview sessions and reports. The results of a
  personality questionnaire or a motivational profile will provide
  an objective counterbalance to face-to-face contact.
• As an insight into the candidate's attitudes, self-image,
  motivation and aspirations. Tests such as the OPQ (Occupational Personality Questionnaire) give candidates' own perceptions of their strengths and weaknesses against the results of a
  sample of comparable-level graduates/managers/directors.
  Candidates are frequently very impressed by the amount of
  detail they receive from the psychologist during the debriefing
  of this type of testing.
• As an indication of the candidate's degree of job satisfaction

and challenge. Some tests can reveal to a client and to the candidate that he/she has slowed on the curve of progression upwards, has plateaued or has just stayed in the job too long. These show that the company needs to discover whether the person should stay at that level, go on secondment, or take steps to change into the fast lane.

- As a way of identifying untapped skills and aptitudes. A person with specific skills, eg, a computer buff, may, through a suitable battery of tests, reveal other capabilities, allowing you to consider promotions in areas other than where that individual has already proved his/her worth. This increases your scope in team development.

- As a way of creating teams with a balanced and broad range of skills. When finding a new member of the team/board/staff, you may decide to organize testing of the existing group to see what gaps you need to fill; which weaknesses need redressing when you are searching for a new person. This experience can have spin-off effects. It can unsettle everyone, and you must be prepared to aid positive thinking, so that the assessments will be used constructively to improve performance. This is a constructive way of acquiring the co-operation of colleagues without making them feel threatened or uncomfortable while you achieve change with the knowledge thus found. Replacing or interchanging people in responsible positions can be discussed and achieved when the job/person profile has been identified and put under scrutiny, eg, a current managing director may be unsuitable for the 'outgoing' requirement of the new Board concept, but the experience may have shown great aptitude for technical management, so an agreed change of post could probably take place with mutual satisfaction.

- As an indication of someone's integrity. There will be certain positions where it is vital to select a candidate who is reliable and honest. Experts in personality testing advise that these techniques cannot guarantee a person's integrity, but that they can give a *rounded* picture of the candidate.

Psychometric testing involves an expensive outlay – but it could help prevent an even more expensive mistake. Out of the hundreds of tests and centres for assessment available, you will need to take advice and use professional consultancy experience to help you choose those which match your company criteria. All testing is confidential and you should guarantee to each individual involved that the resulting information will be secure and private to the minimum number of people throughout the procedure. Candidates should be encouraged to attend the debriefing.

Finding the best

According to the lore of the search and selection consultants (headhunters) 'the quarry should be tracked down, stalked and finally lured into the honey-baited trap without bringing the process to the notice of the outside world'. Chris Partridge (*The Daily Telegraph*).

As already discussed, the first approach will be to have collated the other firms working within the same sector and similar product – sorting out by research who does what in actuality within each group or division. Then the headhunter is able to identify the person who is really carrying out the function in which the client is interested. This is not always the person who holds the job title so sources are used to confirm and convey who the right person is.

This is time consuming and can be an expensive process for the client if the headhunter chosen is not accustomed and well-facilitated to the type of post for whom the search is being undertaken. Therefore the client (*caveat emptor*) must check the real familiarity and track record in the area of that consultant under consideration. Then it is both cost effective and exciting for the search for 'the best' to begin. The client should end up having a difficult choice between the final two or three candidates who have survived the process.

Advertising top jobs in conjunction with a search has been used within the public sector due to the statutory requirement to be seen to have the post open for all. Now the private sector is heading in a similar direction. I have been accustomed to putting both applicants and identified candidates 'in the frame' and taking all suitable people through the process together.

There is an argument, which strengthens or weakens according to the state of the economy, that senior people do not scrutinize advertisements and apply. Conversely, advertising can bring odd candidates into sight about whom nothing would have been discovered through search. The message for the individual is to be alert to advertising in main papers and journals as well as spreading the news about oneself. The danger lies in letting your CV fall into the hands of recruiters who pass it around to other companies without your knowledge and may cause you embarrassment. So do check what will happen to any information you supply through answering an advertisement.

This chapter will have alerted you to the need for personal stocktaking, positive reaction to calls from headhunters and confident self-presentation which when identified will include you among the best for the best jobs.

Headhunters do well when times are very good *or* very bad. In both instances companies and organizations realize that the need for the best people in their senior posts is vital. Hilary Sears of Boyden International, who specializes in marketing directors, maintains that business in the 1990s is being affected by a rapidity of change that is economic, social and political, therefore management must be 'on its toes' – dynamic with a clear adaptable strategy and emphasis on updating marketing constantly.

Sir Allen Sheppard, Chairman of Grand Metropolitan, pinpoints two likely winners in business structures for the foreseeable future: 'One was niche companies responding to special product and geographic opportunities. The other would be big corporations capable of developing and handling brands globally'. A pattern of consolidation is also emerging within the professions such as lawyers and accountants. The implication for the individual is to avoid being caught in the middle range and for the selectors to service clients who are progressing in the successful growth areas.

Executive Search and the European Recruitment Market, The Economist Special Report no 1198 is a useful publication to check the key data for leading executive search firms across Europe. The European dimension is already being discussed, as the basic problems, such as the management of cross-border assignments, minimal co-ordination of client lists and narrow candidate searches, become noticeable.

It is a great advantage to be able to obtain informed advice from people outside your own company and to select senior management on a totally open basis. When promoting from within one's own structure you are selecting from within a limited group in a competitive situation. Some may well be switched off if their reasonable expectations are not met – outsiders are often accepted more easily than working for an ex-colleague.

Using executive search is seen by the client as a professional service and by the candidate as a sign of successful recognition.

Whether you are being selected or making a selection – do not feel nervous or dread the activity. Now you are familiar with the process you can perfect your presentation and judgement. When properly handled selection procedures will enhance your own confidence and your career prospects.

Knowing how to conduct yourself throughout job interviews will open new doors for you as you will be remembered and respected by the headhunters and their clients. You will find that your improved confidence will keep you on the path to the Boardroom which may have eluded you otherwise. Knowing how to make successful appointments will also further your standing and aid in your promotions. You will earn the reputation for being a winner who surrounds yourself with winners.

Part III

· 5 ·

Earning Your Reputation

Your responsibilities grow as you 'go up the ladder'. You have proved yourself as a competent manager and demonstrated a readiness to move up. Your progress from here will require more sophisticated powers of influence, building coalitions with others at your new level and above.

Whether you want to be, or already have been, invited to join the higher echelons – the inner core of the decision making in your organization – you should be well prepared. You will be adding your contribution to the group of leaders, drawn from all levels, who create the work atmosphere and hold the key positions. This could be the point where you have to 'fit in' as well as producing results, and it requires greater insight and different skills from those you have used to date.

By now you will be:

- An enlightened player in power games
- Team building
- Dealing with success
- A mentor
- Entering into advanced self-awareness and the leadership skills you will be using at the top

5.1 DEVELOPING YOUR LEADERSHIP

Leadership styles

Now is the time when you must get to grips with different styles of leadership. Learn that being a leader is *not* about excelling in one, vivid style of leadership. In today's increasingly complex and changing environment, leaders must have a repertoire of styles to suit different organizations, employees, and business environments. It is possible to identify five approaches to leadership ranging from autocratic to democratic styles:

1. At one extreme, you make the decisions yourself using information to hand or easily available in the files, or by desk research.
2. You discuss the situation with others involved, then make the decision on your own.
3. You ask others what they would do in order to solve the problem, then make the decision after hearing their ideas.
4. You favour more teamworking and call the group together, outline the scenario, ask for suggestions, listen to the discussion and then decide on your own. This is after you explain that you are the decision-maker, so each person will be presenting their own case.
5. You prefer a fully democratic style of leadership and call the group together as before – but this time you explain that the outcome will be a group decision. This is participation at its best and agreement may well be mutually successful.

You need to decide which style is the most appropriate for a given situation. For example, when *time* is of the essence, it is quicker to be the autocrat and rule on what you think *should* be done rather than going through a participative discussion. Time is valuable, non-transferable, inelastic and perishable, so whenever possible and you are certain your decision will be accepted (or at least, not opposed) then go ahead and be autocratic.

If time is not a problem, do try to be more democratic. The opportunity to participate and contribute to the decision-making usually gives subordinates a clearer picture of the overall situation and allows them to grapple with some of the dilemmas you and other senior managers are accustomed to contending with. This is good training for them for when they are promoted to policy-making positions.

Whichever style you choose, remember always to present your decisions in an optimistic and cheerful way (giving the good news) rather than a heavy prophesy of doom or saying 'I don't know if this will work'. Doing it this way will increase the chances of quick, confident action from your staff. Letting your people always know where they stand gives you the force to lead.

Project yourself with confidence. Be sure to: smile, say thank you, ask for help, offer help, ask questions and speak up at meetings.

Leadership is – taking responsibility. At King Edward VII school in Birmingham, they start identifying leadership skills from the moment that the children commence.

Management methods

Your management method is a key determinant of your employee's motivation and behaviour. By taking time to consider your particular style, you will be able to consider how you affect their performance. The way you communicate with your staff will demonstrate your effectiveness as a manager. There is no right or wrong way of managing, but there is an appropriate style you can adapt to different situations. In particular, consider how your leadership style affects the type and quality of staff performance. For example, if you adopt the role of mentor to your staff, you will be encouraging them to develop themselves. The less intrusive you are the better they will perform. You will encourage staff to take greater personal responsibility and to aim for high and challenging performance standards and more innovation. In an organization which values these goals, employees will positively respond. Managers and staff will see high rewards and recognition for their contribution, so their morale will be high and they will be motivated to achieve, leading to improved productivity.

A more autocratic style might be more appropriate in an

organization that values speed of work, bureaucratic efficiency, rules and regulations.

By setting administrative rules and procedures, you are training your staff to react immediately and obediently to your demands. This style of leadership is often dangerous however. In today's business world, employees increasingly expect to be consulted about their work. You may find that you are demoralizing your management and staff. They might perceive your leadership as management by fear and accept little responsibility within their jobs. They could decide to behave in an equally reactionary way, work to rule or even go on strike. In any event, they will not be achieving and the organization will suffer from reduced productivity.

In contrast, a more democratic style of leadership can lead to better work relationships but less control over performance levels and standards.

By giving people pre-eminence over tasks you help to create a friendly and open environment. If, however, you overly rely on this as a way of motivating people and give too little direction or control, managers and staff will have little understanding of standards or recognition of task accomplishment. You and your people will not be meeting targets and, again, the organization will suffer low productivity.

The message is that you should equalize job requirements, levels of self-motivation and the competence of the people concerned. With this knowledge, you can then decide on the most appropriate style.

Sometimes you will have to strengthen control systems, other times you will need to be easily accessible as a counsellor, and often you will be the coach. Your success as a leader depends on your sensitivity to what is required at any point in time: you must have your antennae working at all times to pick up the signals. You are working for the common good and thereby increasing the strength of your own pivotal position.

The profiles of successful managers have changed dramatically over the last 40 years. In the 1950s they were preoccupied with operational and production issues. This was followed by management by objectives with central direction and using the autocratic style. The emerging view is that a more creative, flexible and human approach to management will be the predominant style in the 1990s.

Such a change bodes well for women managers, many of whom are still being prevented from moving into senior leadership positions. Current statistics indicate that only 2% of directors in public companies in Britain are women, an abysmal figure. However, as organizations look for a greater variety of leaders, it is more likely that they will value more highly the flexibility and interpersonal skills with which women are often equipped.

Indeed, academic research has revealed that women have some valuable skills to offer.

Since 1922, the American research institution, the Johnston O'Connor Research Foundation Inc., has aptitude-tested more than 60,000 men and women and followed their career development over the years. The Foundation concludes that in ten inborn career talents, there are no differences between men and women. But in six key areas there *are* differences. Women make excellent top managers, given the opportunity, because they are strong in the following aptitudes:

- Abstract visualization – 75 per cent of women were found to be excellent at working well with abstract ideas, compared with 50 per cent of men
- Silograms – women have a talent for acquiring languages and professional terms
- Number memory – women 'are better than men'
- Graphoria – women have good speed and efficiency in number ability, contrary to popular perception. Those who are good are very good
- Observation – spotting small changes in physical detail comes more easily to women than to most men because of women's natural curiosity
- Finger dexterity – the majority of machinists and computer assembly people are women. Unfortunately it is a skill which can keep women at lower levels

Men are better at other aspects of management, such as:

- Structural visualization – the ability to picture solid forms relevant to engineering and mechanics
- Spacial capacity – understanding three dimensional concepts

Therefore, there ought to be at least as many women as men in management level jobs (if not more). In addition to more organizations needing to give women a chance to prove themselves, women need to believe in themselves and know that executive, financial and entrepreneurial ability is *not* the sole preserve of men.

Whether you are male or female, once you become aware of your own style and preferences in leadership, then you have the integral tools for learning and growth, both as a person and as a leader. You will be able to switch methods while retaining your individuality (your individual stamp on a situation) to suit the predicament or strategy.

A leader is someone who stimulates others to a higher level of achievement. In any group, one or more persons will rise to the decision-making challenge and show the steps to be taken to reach the objective. So do you have the capacity to mobilize other people to deal with the task, the competition and sometimes conflict? Leadership is a two-way process, because for every leader there must be at least one listener or follower.

As with high-flyers in general, you have an advantage if you are the first child in the family, because eldest children learn early to achieve and to aim for the top. Coincidentally, being a fourth child also seems to be relevant to being a recognized leader: Napoleon, Nelson, Stalin and Hitler were all fourth children. Eldest children leaders include Alexander the Great, Joan of Arc, Winston Churchill and many others.

Effective thinking

Experts list several traits that help people become effective leaders. One is the ability to mix well with all sorts of people from varied backgrounds – and to be curious about what makes people tick. Those of you who have tried more than one business sector, function or operation before reaching senior management, should benefit from wider horizons. Integrity is an important attribute: to be an effective leader you should have honed the ability to be fair and to be seen to be loyal and reliable.

Today's leaders are also perceived as innovators. When you have ideas, when you are the source of a flow of fresh ways of production or practices in your organization, you become a key player. As an innovator who sees these ideas from concept through to successful application, you have a direct impact on your company's reputation for innovation, entrepreneurialism and market responsiveness. The newer the firm, the greater the likelihood that leaders with these talents will flourish. The more competitive the business environment, the greater need among companies for entrepreneurial leaders. You have a choice of three roles:

1. The creative thinker.
2. The intrapreneur (an entrepreneur in a company).
3. The executive champion (a manager who is able to sponsor or promote both the thinker and entrepreneur).

When you are at the top of the firm and a creative thinker, innovator or champion, then the culture of the organization will be increasingly entrepreneurial. Such firms breed people who are greater achievers, better motivated, more persistent and confident. This is visible by your alertness, sensitivity and keener vision for seeking opportunities, and you will acquire a higher level of awareness when working in such a climate.

Leaders in this type of environment thrive when they accept that their success or failure is essentially in their own hands. By finding an organization which encourages independent managers, you can develop your creativity and entrepreneurial abilities. It is this 'internal locus of control' which identifies the entrepreneurial manager from the solely functional manager. Entrepreneurs are risk-takers with both their own capital and the integrity of their own circumstances – the latter being the most critical. Medium and large organizations provide an umbrella against risk for their managers, and decision-making may be a joint activity with responsibility very rarely at an individual level. To be entrepreneurial, you have to have the chance to take risks, to put both your company and yourself on the line. Companies which allow scope for managerial enterprise encourage their managers to find reality at the cutting edge.

If you are an entrepreneur whose organization has grown quickly due to the success of your product or idea, do try and keep your original qualities intact. Buy in the administrative and management skills that you need for efficiency. Acknowledge that your skills are different and stay in control that way. Each business needs inventiveness and your enthusiasm.

This is when you need to renew the enterprise possibilities and ignore the urge to make everything orderly, returning the focus to the 'small company look'. In medium or large organizations, you can put in informal procedures which make it possible for the next tier of managers to have a chance to operate more entrepreneurially and for the firm to benefit from their ideas, values, determination and persistence.

You need to have agreement at the top that the activities fit into the mission of the company; that when 'failure' occurs there is support and not blame from on high. Management must believe in the philosophy that it is 'better to have tried and failed than not to have tried at all'. Leaders who help to mould the enterprise culture can play a key role in maintaining a vision within the company through keeping their team/company/division encouraged through any stages of uncertainty, ambiguity and, at the end of the day, either success or failure.

How you think is particularly important. Lateral thinking, for example, is a useful tool for senior people. Those who lead usually rise above the mundane, find another angle or shift the emphasis so that problems can be resolved in a way that suits all parties.

Another aptitude common to those 'at the top' is that of having a global view. This means being able to see the big picture, and to fit all the pieces together in the daily management programme to achieve it. These managers are known to have 'helicopter vision' and often prove to be more effective. You should develop looking at the overall layout of situations; the implications beyond your division and how your organization fits into the world scene. This means that you can 'see the wood for the trees' because it means understanding the whole scenario and not allowing all the component parts to grow in importance to prevent the complete scene emerging. This ability peaks between the early teens and early thirties, and is an argument for promoting managers at a young age.

Helicopter vision is useful because it cuts through the concerns and responsibility (and therefore vulnerabilities) which colour an individual's way of regarding projects. If you have children or a large mortgage, for example, you will become more and more concerned with meeting those needs and less able to take a 'helicopter' view. Stop, and check what stage you are at now.

Having a vision is another aspect of thinking differently from managers. When you are heading a company, group or team, you need to have a clear picture of what you want to achieve. A good leader will turn this picture into a detailed vision, which both inspires people and gives them an equally clear sense of the goals, values and purposes of the organization. Each person involved knows exactly what the leader requires of them, resulting in them giving of their best. Leaders are also good at giving employees praise and encouragement, making them feel important and often noting specific details to discuss with relevant staff. Followers are first impressed, and then influenced, by the boss who makes them more aware of exactly what is expected from them in terms of function and target – but who will understand that it is not just the activity which is noted, but also their individual characteristics such as background, promotion in the job, and all those facets which make up the individual personality and shows that he/she is not being regarded as a robot.

You will have gained your reputation from peers and staff as a leader if you are able to give *purpose* to all concerned. By focusing everyone on the tasks in hand, how to do them and how the result fits into the total corporate strategy, you will make petty jealousies, whining and complaints fade into insignificance as everyone is involved in achieving a common purpose or task. You will be able to change your organization as you change the hearts and minds of the people around you.

Successful leaders, whether they lead from in front or behind, will let everyone believe that the tasks and goals have been set by *them* and that their input is valuable. He or she will allow enough time/discussion for each person to grasp fully what needs to be done. The output may be the same as that achieved by a less participative approach but the energy released by a co-operative effort means better quality and speed of operation. You can give purpose by lifting people from their daily preoccupations and letting them glimpse the value of the outcome of their work. Staff who are happy look to you as their leader/manager for more. This is not always a rational process: it is often helped by charismatic delivery and inspirational focus. Simplistically, knowing that you need six times the width of a parcel in string to tie it successfully does not mean that you will always produce a neat parcel.

If you are to exercise any of the above characteristics, such as giving people purpose and being a charismatic leader, you *must* know how to relate to staff. As a senior manager, you are the visible model for those who report to you, for colleagues, and even for those who may be observing you from higher up – or even from outside. You are exposed in whatever you do – take advantage of your visibility and concentrate on gaining the loyalty and respect of your staff. You may choose to be a 'walkabout' manager, with an open door policy, or you may use your time even more usefully by communicating so well with your staff that each is confident in knowing what they are doing and do not need you to constantly bolster them. Your whole impact will depend on your being able to relate to others. You do not have to be always the same – people form attachments by common faults rather than linking to a paragon of virtue who never makes mistakes. Be sure of yourself. Admit mistakes – but only when you have found the solution.

All leaders have used rituals, programmes of activities and reward ceremonies to augment their demands. All religions, political groups and formalized institutions know how to create credibility and adherents by these formalities as well as by informal contact. Use them yourself. Think about how you can use outings, dinners and conferences and other forms of communal activity to help you as the leader to be bigger and more inspirational than your followers. Be believable – be emulated.

Managing groups and teams

Even at the top – even if you are an effective manager and a good leader – you will find it hard to go further in any organization by acting all on your own. The teams above, at your level and below, can all interact and bolster your position.

5.2   UNDERSTANDING GROUP DYNAMICS

Why groups form

In order to make use of and lead teams effectively, you should develop an awareness of why groups are formed, what stages their development goes through and the dynamics involved. There are four dimensions to consider: the individuals involved, the situation within which the group is formed and is operating, how it develops and how the levels of integration influence achievement.

Groups are established at many different levels, from functional ones created to undertake particular tasks or projects (these are usually quite formal) to more informal ones based on friendship or common interests. From the point of view of the organization, you will be trying to ensure that the thinking and activities of the people involved at any one time are related to the overall goals or philosophy of the company/workplace. Often you will need to deal with problems stemming from personality clashes within a group and disappointing group performance.

Each member of the group, including you, will have his or her own personality traits and characteristics which will affect group behaviour as a whole. Each person will have his or her own unique background, physical abilities, level of intelligence and expectations, and the degree of interaction within the group will be affected by what each person is bringing to it.

Where there is a common purpose or task, the group will work better towards a higher level of competence and eventual success. These purposes or tasks can be classified according to whether the emphasis is on production, discussion or problem-solving. Your role in each of these circumstances will be different so you will need to be flexible and adapt your behaviour and leadership style as necessary.

Groups which consist of people with similar profiles will perform better on simple or routine tasks. They will, however, be less creative when tackling more complex issues because they will tend to retain a high level of conformity and not indulge in wider thinking to reach solutions. Though potentially more creative, groups including several dissimilar profiles will depend on your skilful leadership to prevent conflict.

Power fluctuations

Different groups develop at different rates but all tend to follow a similar four-stage pattern which you should understand in order to maximize your influence:

1. Orientation
2. Internal problem-solving
3. Growth and productivity
4. Evaluation and control

All of these stages are dependent on two common features – the behaviour required of the individual contributors and the culture of the organization. Changes in these elements will either accelerate or slow down the rate of movement to the next stage. By careful management and thought, you will be able to interject to effect any changes which you judge necessary.

The immediate response of individuals to a group is usually either agreement, contradiction or eccentric. Provided you, as the senior manager or the person in charge, can be visible and heard, you will be able to ensure that the contributions are leading to the same goals. Giving status or importance to what the group exists to do improves the chances of this happening. Your role is to make sure that the group members perceive their importance and that what and how they perform will be noted and used in the final outcome. You need to persuade everyone involved that the tasks are vital so that each will be willing to give their all. Structuring the tasks so that each person understands the role expected creates a congenial atmosphere in which group members can contribute. Clear guidance from you can help reduce role ambiguity, as well as preventing an overload of work on the few by the many.

The closer and more attractive you make your influence on the group, the more cohesive will be its performance and the less often there will be unproductive competition between group members.

You can help to forge this close influence by emphasizing the value of accomplishing the task, allowing participation in the planning of the strategy, or creating intergroup competitiveness.

You must also get to grips with power, and begin to wield your influence with your staff, peers and superiors. Remember that at every level in your development, there is the capacity for one party to influence the behaviour of other parties to make them act as the first party wants. Make sure you are the first party.

The dimensions of your powerbase will depend on how many people you are able to influence and whether they are above you, below you or at the same level. The scope of your power will cover the number of activities you influence.

When you use power, you are the enactor and other/s are the target/s. Labels (eg, head of division), the ability to reward, the knack of coercing, a fund of information, the facility to recommend – all these things, and others, can invest you with power over other people. They mean you are in a position to *affect* your 'target'. How that person or group will react depends on mutual respect, on the personalities involved and the people concerned, so you have to measure carefully how far you can go.

As always, your power to control will depend on the objectives of all the people in the target area. Your methods of coping with the uncertainty or susceptibility of the receiver will give you the edge on the situation. Your demands will receive co-operation or positive reaction when you are positive and not confused, and you will be using your power to most effect when you are fitting into the strategy or plans already agreed rather than suddenly going off at a tangent or requiring something unexpected.

You can gain your objectives in different ways. Acting as an autocrat and shouting demands is usually less successful (except in crisis or emergency situations) than seeking co-operation by contracting agreements with your staff or those you want to influence, or by gaining their compliance by forming a coalition for a specific purpose, such as agreeing to do something together to solve the problem. This last technique is crucial if you are trying to use your powerbase to keep the organization functioning well. You can create or encourage coalitions between the executive and the bureaucrat, using your expertise to connect action with process – this is how many political decisions are reached.

Some people will comply with your demands in order to be rewarded or to further a good relationship. So, by evaluating the possible reaction of your target, you can improve your power influence.

You will find that conflict in an organization usually arises out of goal incompatibility, or lack of agreement with the decisions made, or because of misunderstanding by individuals of what is required of them. You have two ways of using your powerbase to meet or resolve conflict – being assertive or being co-operative. You must use your judgment when choosing which method to adopt, bearing in mind that your aim is to:

- Encourage competitiveness
- Avoid confrontation
- Allow others to share opinions
- Collaborate with others
- Use compromise

5.3 DEALING WITH SUCCESS

Penalties and pressures

Becoming a leader sometimes exacts a heavy price. Both men and women leaders are operating in highly pressured environments – many are seeing their jobs vanish in the wake of corporate takeovers, or are involved in ferocious competition for promotion, work gruelling hours, struggle to balance their family and professional responsibilities. Robert Kelley, Professor at Carnegie-Mellon University Business School, states that the new generation of executives need to 'gain warrior status at work, they have to be prepared to put in 60/70 hours a week . . . but they are supposed to be equal partners with wives at home, committed to their kids and in touch with their feelings.'

Perhaps, like them, you are realizing what the pressures are doing to you and have decided to move over into 'the sanity track' – you may be tempted to turn down promotions, switch careers or remain in your job, but in each case you are determined to find more time for yourself and your family.

There are still plenty of people who will always put their career first and who remain indifferent to the idea of trying to balance work and other commitments – the people for whom the top job will always be the top goal. By being like this, you risk burnout at an early age, although there are some people who thrive on a knife-edge.

The signs of trouble are hypochondria, sleep disorders and depression – you may suffer these after you have proved your success and perhaps acquired large amounts of money. You could be disillusioned when you achieve your goals and still find that you want ever more to feel satisfied. Many people, when they reach this point, move to a different career, move geographically, or agree to stay at the professional level at which they are comfortable.

If you are very ambitious and accustomed to having the power of decision-making, this disillusionment can trigger a huge identity crisis. There was, for example a spate of London City men leaving and going to remote islands and country areas to indulge in 'The Good Life' in the late 1980s. This was possibly too extreme a change to be really useful to some of them – it is better to consider a less dramatic step.

What does it take to get to the top? Brains, luck and ambition certainly help, but much depends on the company where you are working. Attitudinal surveys show that companies see foreign competition as less of a threat than domestic rivals. (This is ironic – as global management increases, manager mobility decreases.) So less travelling for the sake of international experience should be part of your career plan. As a high-flyer, you will be groomed in marketing, finance and technological change. The emphasis –

at least in Europe and Japan – will be on foreign markets, and competition is forecast to be based on quality and technical innovation. These are the new pressures you will be dealing with, and you will have to decide on your priorities.

This chapter helps you to confront the pressures which surround you and perhaps damage your performance. If you are to survive the race to the top, you need to protect yourself from stress and anxiety. Organizing your life better is often a key way of alleviating stressful situations, so the next chapter looks in detail at time management and whether you are dominated by unhealthy perceptions about time. *Don't* be a victim of burnout. Even if the top of your profession is not perhaps where you eventually go, the choice should always be *yours*. The last thing you want is to be 'derailed' because of over-whelming pressures and spend the rest of your career days wondering what you might have achieved. Cope with stress and become a leader who is good at leading others because you know and understand your own limits.

Coping with fear

Fear can be a major source of stress in your life. It can be induced by your own vulnerability. For instance, mounting bills make earning money essential, so you become more afraid to take risks at work for fear of precipitating dismissal. The threat of the unknown, or just having to do something that you really do not want to do, can increase your tension.

It is essential to confront and eliminate these type of fears from your life. The more you consider something, the more you will become familiar with it, and the calmer you will be. This adds up to giving you the confidence to act with understanding and in the belief that you are able to undertake the task or role.

Try to detach yourself from the problem. Push the fear of it away by not letting it become so important to you that you end up having sleepless nights, or are paralysed into doing nothing about it.

It is very important to acquire the skill of mastering fear – and thus become able to fulfil your dreams. Total mastery may be a lifetime task – but do start early, as practice will make you more likely to find it. Every such effort is worthwhile – it is all part of the process of knowing yourself.

Develop a method or technique for dealing with problems. Be optimistic – it is very easy to get immersed in the doldrums, the downside of what might happen. A colleague doing a big property deal had a promise of the millions which were needed to proceed, and then it fell through. He tried another bank – that didn't work either. Because he believed in the project, in himself, and in its marketability, he persevered. He approached the third bank – this time with even more research and expertise to make him better prepared. He had survived the problems identified by the first two. He got his funding.

By constantly affirming (not justifying) yourself, you will be able to find the solution. Every experience and problem solved is an addition to your store of knowledge. You are increasing your resourcefulness: think, for example, of something which would have fazed you last year and which you hardly notice this year. This all helps to bolster your self-image.

The same thing applies to personal relationships. Attracting others is easy for some. Believing in yourself is infectious – others will be attracted to you because they want to know your secret. The proverbial wallflower is usually a person who is not happy with him or herself. Being apparently over-confident is off-putting too. It is contentment with oneself which is magnetic.

There may be someone you have met that you would like to know better. Do they know? Sitting alone fantasizing is fine, provided you move on to the next stage – discussing it, visualizing the situation – and finally doing something about it.

What will you do if you are rejected, if nothing happens? This is the fear. Face it – remain optimistic. At worst, learn from the experience, working out why you seem to have miscalculated – then carry on. The circumstances may have been the problem as much as you. If you truly want to continue, be persistent. You will learn to base your judgement on the results you get rather than on intellectual reasoning.

Utilizing stress

Your body responds to the pressures and demands put upon it.

This physical response may be activated by voluntary or involuntary reactions to external or internal pressures caused by changes in your life's events, attitudes and thoughts.

Stress is not always negative or harmful. It can be a helpful motivator, an enabler to greater achievement, or a mobilizer of the body's defence to meet life's emergencies. Positive stress can result in increased energy, alertness and enthusiasm. It can be an antidote to boredom and dullness.

Stress becomes negative when overload goes on for a long time and is not remedied. This harmful stress may cause bodily illness or depression and is aggravated if you have a negative mental attitude toward those unfavourable circumstances over which you have no control.

Therefore it is essential to learn how to manage stress so as to diminish its harmful effects and let it work for you in a positive and beneficial way.

The essential feature of learning to cope with stress is to balance how you feel and how you act. Being depressed is also potentially destructive, so it really is important to learn to cope because there will be more and more pressures and stress as you take on more responsibility and decision-making. Not only will this help you to perform better but it will also help you to do everything you can to protect your own staff from unhealthy pressure.

We all have innate needs, desires and longings which affect our behaviour. Most people are constantly trying, directly or indirectly to satisfy the following deep demands:

- To be especially chosen and wanted by someone
- To be of value to someone, to be loved unconditionally
- To be accepted for what you are and not how you perform
- To have two-way commitments – both personally and professionally
- To have meaningful, worthwhile, challenging work which you know is of some significance

Your ability to fulfil all these desires will be exemplified by your answers to the questions which follow from those requirements – and which will cause stress if not answered positively. Does your partner/boss:

- Meet your needs?
- Enjoy your companionship?
- Accept you as a person?
- Never let you down?
- Never disappoint you?
- Never fail to know your needs?
- Never fail to be there when you need him/her?
- Work harmoniously with you?

You can begin to reduce stress by evaluating your lifestyle and looking after your body.

Evaluating your lifestyle
Are you living beyond your limitations – physical, financial or emotional? Are you sure that your goals and values are realistic or have you set yourself impossibly high targets? If your very way of life is causing stress overload, then taking the following steps should help to release you from the bondage of your own expectations and the demands of others:

- Resentment, anger and anxiety are excess baggage which you need to dump. Go to the sources and confront the people on the issues, or seek help to solve the immediate problems which are making you suffer from these attitudes
- Consider your goals and start working on a step-by-step method rather than aiming for the distant high objective which is too difficult to achieve in one go. Relax your perfectionist requirements of yourself
- Check that you are not being driven by someone else's expectations of you and choose what *you* want to do
- When you have time pressure, either negotiate for more time or enlist help to meet the deadline

You can minimize stress by fulfilling your essential body-related needs, as follows:

- Exercise. Under stress your body manufactures adrenalin which acts as your protection. If you are under threat, the

HOW TO BE HEADHUNTED

adrenalin quickly produces the energy which the body needs to escape that danger, eg to run away from an attacker. Your blood flows quicker, the pupils in your eyes dilate so that you can see better, your respiration quickens, increasing your heart rate, and your blood pressure rises. Blood is sent to your head and your brain and away from other organs which do not need it so much at that moment.

Your stress reaction is your automatic body protection system. It is the non-specific response of your body to any demand put upon it. It can be aroused by trouble at work, a person at home, the tough situation you are facing day in and day out. This means that the hormones are being released constantly to a greater or lesser degree. The way to balance it is by exercise.

Exercise will use up your adrenalin, relaxing your muscles which are made tense and tight by anxiety. By running, walking, swimming or whatever, you reduce your blood pressure, heart rate and cholesterol level. It helps you to sleep better, decreases depression and fatigue and increases your self-image and endurance.

- Nutrition. Six out of ten deaths in the USA are thought to be nutrition related. When you are incorrectly nourished, you succumb to stress more easily. It is a matter of urgent priority to eat regularly, properly and effectively. This probably means increasing the proportions of fibre, fish, white meat, fresh fruit and vegetables in your diet.

- Rest and relaxation. All of us need to relax. There are demands and stresses which you cannot avoid, so take some time to recharge your energy. Consciously take 15-20 minutes daily to do nothing – with no demands being made on you and no decisions for you to make. Do whatever makes it possible for you to relax – take the dog for a walk, have a bath, listen to music – anything that takes the tension out of your body. Put some pleasant activity into your week that you will enjoy contemplating and which will refresh you and spur you on.

An unselfish concern for the welfare of others is another essential ingredient for managing the stress in your life. It is impossible to live entirely for yourself and still be satisfied and content: egoism is the supreme enemy of true joy. The very relationships that make up your family life, that make work a place you enjoy going to, are meant to break down your ego – so by knowing yourself you can then give to others, and reduce stress as a result.

Why stress occurs

Stress can be caused by many different situations, some serious, some trivial. One of the major reasons for stress at work is either having too much or too little to do during the day, for example, according to Cary Cooper, occupational psychologist at UMIST, many managers feel stress from the insecurity of not having enough to do and filling in the time trying to look busy. On the other hand, you may have too much to do each day. Trying to balance personal and professional responsibilities may be another obstacle preventing you from getting on top of your job. This can be due to the hours you work, the location, the mobility involved or just the general level of commitment required. Work relation- ships often cause stress: the boss who gives minimal support, competitve colleagues and uncooperative staff can all soon get you worked up into a state of anxiety and frustration.

If you are still working to attain your career goals, you may be frustrated by a lack of challenge and recognition, and a concom- itant lack of career growth and opportunity. You may feel that you have skills or interests which are of value and relevance to your company but not to your present job. This will be exacerbated if you are not advancing as you had planned, if you are being over-supervised or if you are just not receiving enough recognition or appreciation. Perhaps you feel that you have minimal variety in your job or that additional work is often given to you without sufficient consultation or warning. Whatever the cause, all these frustrations will have the effect of de-energizing you in a slow drip-drip way.

Just identifying the cause of your stress may be enough for you to work out your strategy. This could be as simple as taking the option to clarify your job description or the more complex choice of changing your job.

It is not necessary to accept feeling constantly stressed and tired. Your time, your physical effort and mental application within the company structure and within the environment should be satisfactory and satisfying. Commit yourself to identifying what is upsetting you, then determine how to deal with it.

Discussing the problem with your colleagues and perhaps with your boss can be a good way of eliminating it, both for them and for yourself. A joint effort to change something is always the most effective. Often, stress can be reduced through delegation, giving you a more reasonable workload. Also look for new ways of undertaking your tasks. Are you delegating enough? There are so many new aids for production of documents, for routine production and for repetitive work that a simple answer may be to acquire a relevant piece of equipment. Work out the best way to negotiate what you need and set yourself a target time in which to achieve your objective.

Are you utilizing your personal assistant/secretary to the full extent? Plan with him or her how to share more of the load – you may find that he or she will have ideas already and will react positively to being included in your thinking. At home, include your partner in your planning: he or she may well surprise you with support/sharing of solutions and you could find that he/she is relieved to see you tackling issues that have preoccupied you recently. Talk to friends who might be able to provide information and expertise or help with domestic commitments such as looking after children.

Holding a grudge or not having cleared up a disagreement may have created some foes in your mind You do not need this sort of stress. Confront the issue, try and meet with the other person and off-load your opinions, and so clear the air. You will be relieved and consequently be relaxed.

No parent has full-time freedom from guilt. Wondering if the children would be better if the parent was more available is at the back of most parents' minds most of the time. This is especially the case if your company expects you to travel frequently or to work well into the evening from time to time. The guilt which arises from having to change arrangements in your private life needs to be faced. Discover where your priorities lie and plan accordingly. Think about whether a workplace creche would help you and others like you. If so, research into how such an arrangement works (look at the examples of companies such as Midland Bank and Merrill Lynch) and present a detailed proposal to your company arguing your case.

Are you having enough holidays? Breaks or holidays of short duration and at frequent intervals are viewed by the medical fraternity as being of most benefit to the individual. Regular long weekends, week-long holidays and changes of scenery have a great recuperative value – but they are only worthwhile if you train yourself to leave work behind. Use a relaxation or 'switch-off' technique to trigger you into a different mode as you leave the place of work, and don't take work on holiday.

It is worth investing in as much domestic and administrative support as you can. Work out how much you can afford to spend on domestic help, taxis and professional services. The local dry-cleaners, newsagents, caterers, au pair agency, laundry, gardener, decorator, etc, will be glad to be of service! Value your own time and cost your input into the chores to get a realistic understanding of comparative costs without increasing your financial pressures. Then use the time saved to increase your pleasures.

Develop a sporting interest: squash, swimming, golf, jogging or whatever turns you on. If you have not developed an interest yet, now is your chance: clubs and leisure facilities are more accessible now that the population is gradually becoming more health-conscious. More exercise will give you more energy; more energy will reduce the effects of stress.

5.4 MANAGING SUBORDINATES

The atmosphere in the 1990s

The 1990s will be characterized by a desperate hunt for skilled staff, not only managers but also specialists, technicians and administrators. Even now, blue chip companies are recognizing that their future stability and success may be threatened by their inability to find, develop and retain key staff. They are now intensely competing against their rivals to win the recruitment stakes.

What has all this to do with you? Simply put, everything. Your continued rise to the top will be increasingly determined by your performance *and* that of your staff. Your potential as a top executive will be determined by how well you look after these individuals, promote their advancement, develop their skills and deal with any problems that could lead to a dip in performance or talented staff leaving. Organizations increasingly need their most senior people to be skilled at managing staff. They know that the next generation of business leaders will be able to keep their operations cohesive only by inspiring loyalty and commitment among their followers. Begin to learn these skills by seriously considering the personal and professional needs of the people for whom you are currently responsible.

Promoting and encouraging

More and more high-flyers are planning their career development and moves: you will be respected for your encouragement of their aspirations. By responding positively to team members who request experience in an area different from the one you have allocated to them, you will enhance your reputation as a responsive, caring and flexible manager. The company will benefit from the energetic employee who is allowed to work with maximum freedom, and your halo will glow brighter for making it possible.

Don't, however, fall into the trap of expecting your staff to want to follow in *your* footsteps. Try and look at the possibilities through the eyes of the coming generation many of whom may have very different values and aspirations to your generation. You have reached your pinnacle your way and this may or may not be the best way for the managers and staff who are still seeking development and promotion. They *may* be seeking to follow in your footsteps, or they may want to achieve even more, so your role is to make the opportunities as wide as possible. Your reputation depends on the outcome of the future careers of those for whom you are responsible as much as on your success today.

What do you do, however, with the team member who does not seem to be going anywhere? Just because someone has stayed with the company for ten or 15 years and shown their loyalty may not mean that they are maximizing their potential. Be careful not to fall into the trap of tolerating an average performer because of habit and familiarity. Try to stimulate such people into developing their plans for the future, and help them to make a start on implementing them. Whatever you do, avoid trying to shape up these people by giving them responsibilities that they cannot cope with. The 'Peter Principle', where someone is promoted to the level of their incompetence is a familiar problem. Don't leave behind a legacy of such appointments as you progress up the career ladder.

A major way of making sound developmental and promotion decisions about your staff is to introduce some kind of formal evaluation system. An enlightened head of an organization and the Board or decision-makers should support you if you decide to introduce regular performance appraisals for your people. This practice is widely accepted, indeed ambitious individuals now expect to be noticed regularly in this way. They have a mature understanding of how appraisal can be treated as an invaluable opportunity to have open, two way discussions about the appraisee's future in the organization. Emphasize this to your staff and also point out that formal appraisal encourages performance. This will encourage Board's members to keep an eye on those showing promise, as well as in those who are leaving the job as part of a planned career move.

All this will show people in your organization that you are determined to ensure your section maintains its vitality through management development programmes. The balance of retaining people who are performing well and bringing in the enthusiastic newcomer with other experience, will keep your operation successful. It is only when your people have not had a promotion within your domain, even with management development facilities available, that you may need to make the difficult decision to move them on (if they have not realized their situation already) so that you are not back into the 'average performance dilemma' again.

Fixed-term contracts may aid your endeavours to stimulate people and prevent these difficult decisions arising. Renewable contracts suit second and third tier management and keep them on their toes to deliver within a given period. However, the contract-holder knows that it is OK to go elsewhere at the end of the contract and may plan accordingly. This will not always suit you.

The relatively recent fashion for early retirement at the top accelerates progress: you know that you are not in your post ad infinitum and need to keep planning ahead. This is a stimulus to stay visible, to keep your reputation growing through your own and your staff's performance, even after you believe that you have arrived.

Focussing on health

More and more companies are beginning to recognize the managerial and cost-effective benefits of health care, checks and promotion. They know that their workforce is too vital an asset to be neglected and that time and money spent in counselling and healthcare can represent enormous savings in terms of human energy, talent and productivity.

In general, US firms are at the vanguard of employee health. British firms are a little shy of following their example, as Cary Cooper and Deborah McInerny of UMIST point out. They comment: 'The average Brit would recoil at Americanisms such as "Worksite Wellness", "Live for Life" programmes and the SANE (Smoking, Alcohol, Nutrition and Exercise) approach to worker well-being. But this concept of health promotion at work saves the US millions of dollars every year in reduced absenteeism and sickness benefits'.

But attitudes in the UK are changing. A recent discussion with a colleague who specializes in outplacement counselling (where an individual's employer pays for them to receive help to find and keep another job) revealed that employers are beginning to seek professional help to deal with employees suffering from emotional or physical problems. Alcoholism and drug abuse (from valium to cocaine) are high on the list of requests for help. My own research reveals that in 1988–89, a high percentage of UK companies (around 80 per cent provided access to medical checkups – but two-thirds of this provision is available to management only. There are some enlightened companies (about ten per cent) who have annual checks for all employees. Of course, many of these companies are Japanese owned. We may smile at their early morning exercises and medical provision for employees – but they are not just being paternalistic, they are being extremely shrewd and have one eye on the profitability of an enterprise with a happy, healthy workforce.

The question of healthy working environments is being debated more often. The sick building syndrome which emerged after outbreaks of Legionnaires disease in Britain promoted a wider media focus on such evils as faulty air conditioning, faulty water cooling systems, flickering fluorescent light, static electricity from floors and ceilings, and the chronic lack of well-being they could cause to people working within those walls. You can ask your local environmental health officers to check out your controls and equipment – if they have not contacted you already. Your staff will appreciate any remedies you can introduce, and you will appreciate the increased output.

Smoking is no longer the vexed question it once was. Generally speaking, there is wide acceptance of non-smoking areas/offices/ buildings now that there is public acceptance of the prevalence of its ill effects. About 20 per cent of UK companies have a 'no-smoking' policy, whether formally or informally practised. Like the airlines, industry and commerce has discovered the savings in cleaning bills as well as the value of helping those who do not smoke or who wish to kick the habit. However, there are very few resources allocated for support systems for those who suffer withdrawal symptoms – which can be both debilitating and severe. When you are encouraging people, your understanding of the need to support any individual trying to improve or change his or her lifestyle and habits will earn you gratitude.

There can be a conflict in the policy of encouraging staff to meet informally in the company bar after work: the idea of everyone getting to know each other better is grand, but the temptation for the 'boozers' is huge. Just under 50 per cent of company premises have a bar provision yet the effect of alcohol problems on work is well-known. Paradoxically, by pretending that such problems don't exist, companies get poor returns on this staff facility. You must consider such problems and take steps to help those affected. With drugs, you will find it more difficult to identify the culprits (the sources) and the victims (the addicts) and, most likely, you will need the assistance of outside agencies to help those involved.

Stress management seminars, workshops, how to cope books and counselling are top of the popularity stakes among employees whenever provided, yet more than half of corporations still push the problem of emotional ill-health under the carpet and ignore the need to help. You will find that where work-system changes, multi-tier regular training or redevelopment programmes are put into the work routine, less employees suffer from stress. This in turn feeds into the team or department; group dynamics, atmosphere and production visibly improve. Those companies who are known to have employee health-care on the agenda (Kelloggs, Scandinavian Bank, the Post Office, British Telecom, Shell UK) all believe they benefit in some way from a fit workforce.

5.5 KEEPING THE BEST

No matter how carefully organizations select their people, there will always be appointments which simply do not work. This can be for a variety of reasons, some of which become instantly apparent, such as technical or managerial incompetence, some of which are less obvious, for example staff who reach a plateau in their work and who 'psychologically retire', or those who fail to adjust to the corporate culture and who hold inappropriate or conflicting values and attitudes. Whatever the reason, it is your responsibility to handle the problem sensibly and carefully. Above all you *must* respond quickly as staff who are unsuitable can cause waves of frustration throughout your team or department, resulting in division and factions.

Achievement indicators

There is the stage when an individual feels their career is static;

that they are unlikely to be promoted further within their company and that their job satisfaction and challenge is nil. In some larger companies, this can happen to up to 50 per cent of managers, and can include a number of people who had been considered to be high-flyers earlier on in their careers. In order to avoid this happening, you need to ensure your staff are constantly updating their skills so that they always have some marketable commodities to offer.

In their quest to promote the best possible people, many companies now set their staff performance targets which get more and more difficult and challenging. Obviously, some of these employees will reach a point where they cannot achieve these targets. However, many companies have alternative career paths prepared for those managers who level out. This way they still benefit from their experience and the investment in training and development.

In your senior capacity, you should make similar contingency plans for people down your lines of management so that hard working and valuable employees do not feel they are on the rubbish heap. You should build in training programmes that aid sideways moves as often as vertical ones. This way you will be keeping the calibre of your middle managers intact while promoting those who still have more to offer. It is now recognized that because someone has peaked on one path does not mean that their skills should go to seed. They can be moved to positions that stimulate them afresh and draw out new talent and energy.

When breaking the news to your subordinates that they are not ready for the move upwards and that they may be well-advised to consider a change in direction, you need tact and an understanding of the stage of life through which they are passing. Those who have reached their forties will probably resent your suggestions most: they may well have been planning to reach board level ever since they started working and assumed they could get there in a straight line – being thwarted will be hard for them to take. The revelation will be less painful to those in their thirties, for two main reasons – they are less likely to have been indoctrinated with the belief that the only way forward is upwards and they will feel that they have time to develop in another direction. Younger people's values are often less materialistic and include the fulfilment of personal and intellectual needs as well as financial ones. They will probably be more open to career moves that offer personal development.

Dealing with plateaued staff prevents you or your staff from being ensnared by the false belief that the only way to progress is vertically through the organization with the inevitable result that everyone is eventually promoted beyond the level of their competence. Secondment or lateral moves within or without the company are now much more highly regarded as a means of continuing to stretch and challenge staff.

You have the responsibility of using such means creatively to align the goals of the individual with those of the company. Properly planned, you will aim to find ways of enabling each and every employee to work to the best of their ability – whatever stage they have reached in their jobs. Ensure you establish an annual performance appraisal system. This way you can discuss with staff their justification for pay rises, as well as measuring their progress. The easy way to prevent unwelcomed surprises about lacklustre performance is to have quarterly reviews.

Don't forget that specialist staff can be affected by plateauing too – so even if you have a highly experienced research biogenist, beware, he or she too needs to avoid over specialism. Encourage your specialist staff to develop more mainstream skills as well, particularly general management, so that they can adapt easily if their demand and circumstances change.

You may find that managers, and even yourself, could be re-invigorated by switching direction. The company gains benefit too – from feedback from senior and middle management – so it may even be decided to redesign a job.

If you find yourself or your staff being put in the position of 'being put out to grass', then you/they need to move on. When your organization reduces pay increases, stops paying bonuses and minimizes the availability of training and development, then you are being 'boxed' and have little control over your situation. High flyers are particularly vulnerable and need to be on the alert as a policy change can mean they reach a plateau at a relatively early stage in their careers. This can be indicative of financial crisis within the organization and not necessarily be a reflection on your abilities.

When managers are plateaued or stick at a level in mid-career, those who do not follow the actions already stated will probably put their energies into activities outside work. However, there is one other alternative (according to management experts) and that is the idea there is nothing wrong with being on a plateau provided you look at ways to expand your role at the level you are at.

Biting the bullet

Most people find firing people the hardest task they have to do. It is the *mechanics* of dismissal which probably distresses you most. The emotions you will feel are difficult to cope with, but at least you will know that what you are doing is in the long-term interests of both your company and probably the individual employee as well.

The key to firing anyone is to do it when it suits you and not them. Always have your damage control plan in mind (this can include replacement). You do not want to upset the organization or lose clients, so you must think through the methods you will use. Patience does pay off – even if you have to wait for days, weeks or even months.

However at the time of dismissal it may well be in the company's interests to ask the employee to leave at once – thereby minimizing the possible impact this will have on those around him or her.

There are no rules as to where the firing takes place. It is more considerate to do it in private, but if you really want to get a message across to other employees, you may decide to be more public. You have to rely on your own judgement and to remember that you still have to lead a workforce which may have reactions which you will have to deal with later.

Dismissal is a legal minefield through which you must tread carefully unless you wish to deal with the results of an explosion. 'Few employers understand the importance of observing the proper procedures of dismissal', says Janet Gaymer, expert on employment law and partner of Simmons and Simmons. She advises sticking to the following guidelines to preserve your company from litigation:

- It is inadvisable to ask someone to resign on the assumption that the employee *wants* to leave
- Giving someone the option to resign rather than being dismissed may seem to be a way of solving your problem – but you could be seen to be applying unacceptable pressure from a legal point of view
- Advising someone to find another job then announcing that they are leaving constitutes wrongful dismissal unless the employee concerned has agreed freely that he/she wishes to leave
- The confusion between unfair and wrongful dismissal is something you should be aware of

Because of the issues in this particular field it is far wiser to leave the details of dismissal to the Personnel Director and/or Legal Adviser.

Earning your reputation through your leadership and management of others is how you earn their respect and prove your value to the organization. You increase your achievement and power when you understand group dynamics and make your moves accordingly, then you will be able to deal with your success.

· 6 ·

Holding on to Your Reputation

6.1 NETWORKING

Talking to people

Getting to know people is always both scary and exciting. Your
success will depend largely on your expectations of different
social situations. I believe in the necessity of being alert, of being
aware of the opportunity as it arises and recognizing the links as
they add together to lengthen the chain of contacts.

Originally, we are brought up to be polite, self-effacing and
aware of the dangers of the unknown. We can all remember our
mothers and teachers warning against the stranger. As adults we
have to adjust to discerning when to be cautious and when to be
brave. In any gathering, you may have to open up and say hello
when no one else seems to be saying hello to you. This is one way
of creating business, career and social opportunities: holding
back, being shy and standing back is not the way to develop
knowledge of others.

This final chapter discusses how you hold on to the reputation
which you have carefully constructed, maintained and proved to
be worthy of.

You will continue to build on your abilities and let others know by networking. This will also keep you up to date with the conditions in the marketplace as it is a two way connection. The combination of networking, effectiveness in your company/ organization, time management and your survival strategy will keep you on track so that you can fulfil your future expectations.

> *'People must stop thinking in terms of having, or not having, a job. Instead we should have a portfolio of skills and activities, some for sale, some as gifts. The portfolio might include wage or fee work, from cleaning to conveyancing, homework and child rearing, gift work done voluntarily and study work, training and preparing for a new skill. We shall have to do the balancing ourselves.'* Charles Handy – visiting Professor, London Business School, *The Age of Unreason.*

In the UK we have been taught that it is proper to be introduced. Use a mutual friend to do this whenever possible, and do the same for your friends when you are the host, or in a position to do so – giving a thumb-nail sketch of likely common interests.

Whenever you find yourself alone, having to speak for yourself, say your name clearly, repeating the other person's as soon as you can in the ensuing conversation, as an aid to memory. If business cards are exchanged, do note on the back of the new acquaintance's card some item of place and meeting or appearance, etc, which will jerk the person into your vision when you want to use the contact.

If you play the waiting game – waiting for the other person to speak first – you risk missing meeting the person you really want to meet. Often you will be sidetracked or interrupted – so do practise being in 'the right place at the right time' to make your move. It is no longer considered being pushy to stretch out your hand and introduce yourself. In church services nowadays, there is often a time allotted for the congregation to greet their neighbours: one can form some lasting friendships from this small beginning.

What if the other person does not respond – or even turns away? Rejection! So what? Either you walk away, or you try again. In business, very few people will be so overtly hostile or rude, so it is a risk well worth taking.

What about the complication of approaching someone who may interpret your action as a pass – as a sexual approach (which it may be!)? We are not used to touching in Britain, although it is commonplace in many European countries. It is probably less risky, therefore, to keep initial approaches to a handshake and stating your name when you say 'hello'. Body language is now an area of well-developed and skilled observation, but do not miss out on meeting someone because you are wondering how they will interpret your approach. Be clear about your *thinking* and take it from there.

If you like yourself, believe that you are worth knowing and that it is fun and useful to get to meet other people, then you will find it easier to greet others. It is easier the more often you do it, and your new friends and acquaintances will appreciate your efforts. Making excuses is a negative exercise – we are all good at justifying being the wallflower, being self-contained, and waiting for the other person to move first. Be different, be the one to take the risk and be friendly. After all, you may appear to be standoffish or ignoring the other person if you are just standing there – so go ahead and introduce yourself.

Do include the peripheral person who seems to be excluded into the group if you can. You do not have to be raucous or 'the life and soul of the party' to put yourself forward discreetly and effectively. Go on, you will survive. The more positive you are, the bigger will be your address book.

Every event, however unpromising, can be made to be enjoyable and productive if you plan and practise beforehand. It is an example of positive thinking.

I was in the middle of moving house and various related upheavals, when I suddenly remembered that I had promised to take an old friend to a posh lunch at the House of Commons. I did not feel like making the effort, but neither did I want to let her down, so I went. After finding the packing case with my clothes, dashing to the hairdressers, driving there and parking the car, we arrived just in time.

This was the occasion when I met the man who was to be my boss: yes, I was headhunted to be a headhunter. If I had not kept to the arrangement, I might not have had an exciting career change.

So you never know what can happen from a chance meeting at any time. Of course, there is no guarantee that each committee meeting, reunion, family gathering, cocktail party or whatever will be fruitful – but you won't know if you haven't gone in the first place.

Whatever your status at work, if you are comfortable with yourself, others will be drawn towards you. I dread walking into a room full of strange faces and look to see if I can recognize just one person. If there is someone to whom I can anchor if I feel lost, it is much less difficult. Otherwise I latch on to the nearest open group and beam. After introductions, neutral topics, such as the reason for the event, lead on to more mutually relevant ones.

You can never prophesize just when business or career opportunities may arise. When asked, 'Would you like to come to the pub for a drink after the meeting?', do go – much of the real business of that committee/group/division may be happening informally during these sessions, and in this way you might find out where the actual power base is.

Know your neighbour as yourself. The person to whom you are talking will notice if your eyes glaze, or if you are constantly looking over their shoulder or seeking a way to escape. Treat others as you would like to be treated. The Queen Mother has a reputation – and the love of everyone who meets her – for her concentration on the person to whom she is speaking. It may be a learned technique for you at first, but is is well worth learning – it pays dividends.

If you have the benefit of a large family circle, you will have been learning the technique all your life. Friendship grows with nurturing, and getting to know others anywhere at any time will match your ability to be friendly. Sincere interest shows – so does insincerity. There will always be those who don't respond, but the majority of people cannot resist others' interest in them – it is to be hoped that they will reciprocate by being interested in you.

If you are too gushing or overwhelming (in other words you are not gauging your effect on the other person) they will remember the incident with a negative impression. You will remember those who had had this effect on you, which is not going to encourage you to keep in touch or contact, even if the information or contacts they have could be useful. So beware.

This can also happen if someone has responded to you with a 'put-down'. Being self-important or disparaging of the other person and their status, or not listening properly, is sheer bad manners.

Good manners are not old-fashioned, they are the tools of networking. They start with basic behaviour, such as being punctual, wearing appropriate clothes for the occasion, saying thank you to the host, not drinking too much, allowing others to contribute to the conversation, not ignoring anyone who has a disability, or including someone who is less well-equipped socially. They continue with remembering people on meeting again, which helps you to follow up the useful connections you have made.

Another common danger of networking is when someone is too pushy in using the contact made with you. Someone may pester you, try to sell you something or to use your contacts for his/her own ends. Cross such people off your lists. Don't be guilty of this pushiness either – good manners and good sense will make you good friends and you must accept that you cannot rush this process or try to exploit it.

Being prepared

Keep your CV up to date: you never know when you may find it necessary to produce one in response to a request, or on meeting someone who might tell you about a possible job opportunity. It is also a way of reminding yourself of what you have learnt and cultivated.

For any gathering or event, you need to dress properly, take your wallet and invitation, and complete any travel arrangements. Having a bad day at the office, a row on the way there, bad news or other disasters can be ameliorated by going into automatic gear on arrival. (This pre-supposes that automatic gear exists, so prepare in advance and you will thank yourself when an emergency arises.) This is simply a trick for making sure that you have a positive attitude regardless of the circumstances. If, however, there is a really disastrous situation which you find impossible to shake off, and you are about to be involved with people who may influence your career, don't go. This is only *in extremis* – and make sure that it is not going to cause anyone to be out of pocket, or inconvenienced. If you are the chairperson, the speaker or the host, accept that you *must* be there.

By working out the value of the group with which you are networking, you will be better able to be dynamic company and enjoy the time spent there. The value of the event might involve anything from just being visible to making contact with someone who never returns your calls but is going to be there. Remember that subtlety in approach helps: don't dive straight towards your target, but just 'happen' to be in close proximity at some point during the evening.

Going to the staff party, the PTA meeting, the charity event, the conference or the wedding of your colleague all require different planning and preparation. You will reap benefits from taking presents; knowing names, issues, recipients, professionals or political implications. It is no longer regarded as social climbing to know who people are and what they do or are perceived as doing. Volumes such as *Who's Who*, *Compass*, *Times 500*, *Trade Association* and other year books are some of the invaluable directory-style books in the library which will keep you from making a faux-pas.

An occasion may evolve quite differently from what you had envisaged – take the chances as they arrive. You will have gained confidence from your planning and from some understanding of what might arise. If it happens that you get sidetracked into something entirely different, often out of a conversation early on, then follow on from there, unless your original thinking is even more important and likely to be even more enjoyable. Don't become rigid in your movements because what you had *expected* to happen gives way to something else.

Look at people when you are talking to them, speak clearly and ask them to repeat what you didn't hear properly. 'It is a pleasure to meet you' should be meant. Fill the gaps in conversation as naturally as possible, but don't feel that burden is yours alone – others should be able to do their bit too. Some small talk items stored away are very useful to fall back on at that stodgy cocktail party or whatever. Remember what was the reaction when you tried them at that dinner party before – and weigh up the chances of that happening again.

It is expected that when people are invited to something, they will sing for their supper. You will have been included to add to the occasion – not just by your presence but for your contribution to the conversation, platform, discussion, etc. A new member is given time to acclimatize, but will not be regarded as an asset to the group if they do not make any indication of their thinking. An amusing companion, colleague or guest will always be welcome and remembered. Those who are silent, hoping to be invisible, or aggressive, are not likely to be included regularly.

I have made a conscious effort recently to remember to shake hands when meeting clients or others, and again when leaving. It is amazing how often I forget. I have discovered that it is a useful formal way of cementing the connection made. Men are often surprised when a woman says 'good-bye', 'thank you' or 'I'll be in touch', and then stretches out her hand for a handshake. I find it is a positive way of completing the business.

I first discovered 'kissing the air' when I was in the USA. It had become commonplace to greet people of either sex with one or two cheek kisses, but this has now been perfected by people who are greeting many people often by simply touching cheeks slightly and kissing the air. It makes good sense in the 1990s – and is a continuation of the more gregarious European greeting, so don't be surprised if this happens to you. Business kissing has non-sexual implications – and takes place when meeting out of the office.

Introductions and connections

Networking is about introducing people to others, which is especially useful for both horizontal and vertical integration. That means meeting people at the same professional level, as well as those either above or below.

If you are involved in organizing the event, it helps to be in a position to greet people, to get to know them and to make sure that they are able to meet others quickly and easily. By keeping an eye open during the proceedings, you can help those who are stuck too long in one group, or who are isolated, to meet others. When introducing, give some information as well as the name: items such as the organization they represent or an activity or interest for which they are known are helpful. It is also an opportunity to introduce people with mutual areas of interest.

If you are a guest, try and go with someone you already know or arrange to meet them at the event – but make it possible for both of you to circulate and meet up from time to time rather than sticking together like limpets all the time – thus making it harder to meet people and for others to meet you. You can introduce each other to people you have met before with enthusiasm and positive statements such as, 'This is John who works with me on the project I was telling you about last week. He is the person who had the original idea.' Then the conversation will continue.

When you are looking around to find someone to talk to, there will always be others more nervous than you. Try and put them at their ease by making an approach, explaining who you are and why you are there. This gives them a chance to respond similarly and the ice is broken.

When two people are having an intense conversation, it is best to leave them to it. They will not welcome an interruption, so move on and attach yourself to a bigger group. It is equally difficult to move on gracefully when circulating. Those who are less accustomed to circulating may wonder if they have been boring or said something wrong if you leave too abruptly. If the conversation is one-to-one, try to give some reason for ending it, for example, 'Oh, there is Mary, I must ask her if she wants a lift home'. If possible, bring the other person with you to meet her; if not, make sure he or she can have a way to talk to someone else.

When leaving the gathering, say good-bye to the host. Once you have said you are going, do go: long goodbyes are tedious and awkward for others. If you haven't managed to find the person who invited you, as sometimes happens at a corporate or large affair, do follow up by phoning or writing to that person the next day or very soon afterwards – this helps to keep you on useful mailing lists.

In business and social gatherings, it is becoming less and less usual for people to smoke. Check carefully for an ashtray before lighting up and first ask your companions if they mind. It is important when eating formally to wait until after the loyal toast has been given, and even then to check if it is acceptable.

A good networker will know the times, locations, transport and people involved in any operation where meeting people takes place. Knowing the nearby stations, restaurants, pubs, hotels and related business places gives you the confidence to suggest further action if the need arises. For the self-employed, independent, consultant or freelance professional, these are most important adjuncts to doing business. If a contact has been established to the extent that you want to continue the discussion after the event, be aware of places to go to do this.

Chance meetings often occur when travelling. The person sitting next to you in the aeroplane might just happen to be in your area of business. Be alert (but not too high in your expectations) every time you have to leave home: coincidences and beneficial meetings can and do happen, but not necessarily when you are looking for them.

The same is true of sports and holidays: by following interests and activities you get to know others with similar habits. The more talented you are at tennis, golf or sailing, the more venues, competitions and social activities occur. Who you will meet there depends on your skills and choice of club. Conversely, your circle of friends and colleagues may have influenced or helped your membership in the first place. It is well known that many deals are struck on the golf course, where do you do yours?

The level at which you pitch your spare time activities and holidays will be affected by your income, ambitions, and personal preferences. Some people would rather have a weekend at a grand hotel instead of several weeks at a cheaper place; others may prefer the outdoor life. You need to balance your objectives against your activities. Getting to know people during leisure hours is now as effective and fulfilling as elsewhere. Making friends, which is the core part of networking, cannot always be planned or be part of a strategy, but can be developed for mutual benefit and should always be for fun.

Making contacts

The best networking is a combination of planned contacts and chance encounters. No one will benefit if you are not able to take advantage of the contact, or to help. So, in summary, here are your guidelines to raising your awareness of opportunity:

- Join clubs, go on committees, attend associations
- Have confidence in yourself
- Use appropriate presentation for the circumstances
- Be comfortable in company
- Develop good preparation, knowledge and experience
- Whenever invited to something – go!
- Circulate when you are there
- Speak when in company
- Understand your own objectives
- Know how to behave
- Follow up contacts
- Keep in touch
- Give reciprocal help when possible
- Be friendly and open to new friendships
- Use leisure as well as work time
- Be accessible to friends and colleagues
- Use smart business cards
- Have a telephone answering machine
- Share information
- Always say thank you

When asked about what has contributed to their success many chief executives listed social skills as one of the most important assets. These were usually acquired early on in their lives: many by the age of 20; most by the age of 29. They confirmed that social skills were usually the outcome of having been put amongst other people, and just having to learn to cope (at school, college, on the playing field, etc).

Being able to communicate with people is essential for your own personal and professional development. This 'personal connection' means:

- Being curious about people
- Listening to people
- Being aware
- Being 'in the mood' for socializing
- Explaining reactions
- Taking risks
- Being part of a group/team
- Stating different viewpoints without fear of others' reactions
- Following the winners

When you have these talents or traits, you are well on the way to having social skills which you can use in any situation which is likely to arise.

Women are particularly vulnerable to being summed up by how they are dressed. Men should be aware that there are many nuances in their style of dressing too. Nowadays the 'formal casual' style is the most tricky. Good quality clothes and well-polished shoes help in most circumstances. It is well to check beforehand if you are unsure how formal an occasion is going to be.

When formal invitations are issued, make sure that you reply to the RSVP. Even when less formal, if you say you are coming, do try and attend. If it is not possible, telephone as soon as you know. It is not good practice to assume that you will not be missed. Even where large numbers are expected, you would be surprised how an individual absence is noted. You may not know it but someone may have come particularly to see you or to introduce you to someone they know.

There are particular methods of behaving on certain occasions, such as Ladies Day at Ascot or any place where Royalty is attending. Be sure what the format is and follow the rules. Some corporate functions have their own style too, so as well as reading up on recent transactions and personnel, find out what will be expected of you when being entertained. Some companies, for example, provide transport, and you need to know where you will be collected from and how. It is a good idea to link up with the people in the company at a similar level to yourself for the main activity: this shows recognition of status but will also further your networking.

At trade shows and company conferences you should have plenty of cards, plenty of knowledge, plenty of business development ideas and plenty of smiles. You will function better if you are not concerned with what you have left behind at home or in the office, so do organize well in advance, then you will be free to concentrate on the business in hand.

Corporate networking

You can increase your networking potential by frequent mobility from job to job, either within the company or from company to company. In the more entrepreneurial companies, managers are given the opportunity to move quite often, even if the changes are often lateral rather than vertical. In some enlightened corporations, managers can interchange within functional areas, eg from finance to manufacturing production, or from personnel to operation and thus gain experience. It does not take long under these conditions to establish relationships with peers in many parts of the company – with a series of moves for a group which has worked together originally, each person soon has a close colleague in another part of the organization and so you can call on your colleagues for real support, extra information or backing. The more frequent the moves and the more widely dispersed the original group, the more widely information can, potentially, circulate.

Those of you who move clearly have an advantage over those who don't. You can find out more easily about career opportunities whereas those who don't or can't move are handicapped by their limited access to networking. If you consider each colleague as part of a network spreading over many sectors, and keep in touch, you will be picking up new connections continuously. Organizational communication, knowledge and use of power is increased according to the level of mobility of its people. Mobile people become more cosmopolitan and less biased due to new experiences – however, instabilities do appear when people know they will be constantly on the move. So a good company will make sure that you find change and opportunity not a threat, and that it will be coupled with basic overall security.

Making a lasting impression
It is not a myth that first impressions linger: how you present yourself on first meeting may be the key to future developments.

6.2 TIME MANAGEMENT

How do you use your time?
Are you a day-dreamer, wandering through life as though in a daze, doing things at random, making illogical choices of activity? If so, others will know that you are unpredictable and will treat you accordingly. You will probably not like the discipline of planning or prioritizing so will frequently find yourself in a chaotic state. You will pretend that you find this way of life stimulating and creative: the real problem is that you are frightened of order and routine.

The result will be that you let your abilities trickle away and your dreams remain unfulfilled because you are willing to go though the unpleasant process of trying, failing and trying again. Maybe one day you will wake up and discover that you are not really happy in this mess. You might even begin to tidy up your life, small piece by small piece and see if you like it, and then go on and achieve more.

See if you recognize yourself in the following examples of different ways of perceiving and using time.

Time as your servant

If this is you, you are always hoping that the fairy godmother will come along and rescue you from a life of drudgery; that you will easily realize your dreams and that everything will be made all right for you. You keep procrastinating and telling yourself that you will get round to things eventually. You do not admit to the fact that it is only you who can provide the time you need to tackle those dreams. You are inclined to have a lot of faith in the idea of 'the right time' to make your moves. In fact, you are expert at putting things off for the very best reasons – you live in the wrong area, your boss is not receptive, your excuses are endless . . . Forget them. The right time is now, Begin.

Are you a balancing artist?

If this is you, you are an effective, achieving person who develops at your own pace. You are inclined to respect yourself enough to switch off when the circuits are overheated. Your ability to manage time is impressive, but you are smart enough to know that the best decisions are never made in an atmosphere of pressure. You are not upset by deadlines and your work seldom puts unbearable demands on you – you look ahead and plan the crisis out of existence. You enjoy the steady progress towards success but you could be sidetracked just making things happen. Spend a little more time on the very long-term planning to keep everything really in balance.

Are you an achiever?

This is the level of time management usually attributable to superman/woman. If this is you, you have proved frequently that you know how to get a job done – in fact you prove this all the time. You enjoy cramming a massive amount into each day and in demonstrating how good you are at doing that. You will have had a breakfast meeting or aerobics class before work and go straight from the office to the theatre or a gig with a client. You are compulsive about making each minute matter. Your tolerance of others who are slower reduces as your rate increases. *Relax:* you are about to crash out under this level of stress, so take a look at the balancing artist and see if you can be more like that.

The most important element in an executive's business life is time. It is the only thing of which there is a limited amount, so finding a way of maximizing the use of each hour within the 168 hours in the week is fundamental to your success.

Sometimes time flies, sometimes it crawls: the old saying that 'a watched kettle never boils' is familiar to us all. You can understand the elasticity of time from experience but you can also plan how to use time to give you the maximum scope for doing as much of what you want to do, think and produce as possible. Try to avoid the following 'time traps'.

Time as your master

Beware of the urge to abdicate responsibility for your actions because you bow to the dictates of time. People who give up doing something – like going to a party or taking a journey – because of the time involved, end up missing out on experience. So when you find you are beginning to conform to rigid, clock-linked personal habits, or that you stick to your pre-determined schedule regardless of interruptions or circumstances, you miss out on opportunities of having a more relaxed routine. When you rely on the clock rather than other cues to determine what you do, for example, insisting that all meetings should last exactly one hour, you forego the opportunity of unlooked for developments and opportunities.

Being bound by time limits your choices. Life may appear to be easier as a result, but you will be blocking your opportunities for spontaneity, growth or even professional breakthroughs. By allowing time to be your master, you are relegating your values and goals to second place.

Time as your enemy

Trying to 'beat the clock' puts you in an aggressive frame of mind, and doing this continuously builds up your stress level. Even when you win by completing within the allotted span or gaining minutes here or there, you are still perceiving time as your enemy. This is the scenario within which you may find yourself setting yourself deadlines, or taking shortcuts either in journeys or in work processing. You will end up rushing at your own instigation, not for other necessary reasons.

You will feel triumphant about being early and beaten by being late. The habit of relating to time will become more important than the task in hand. You will strongly resent others who are not so time-orientated, and be upset by others' casual observances such as 'We have plenty of time,' or 'It's OK, there is no need to rush!' Learn to judge yourself and others by the *use* of time rather than adherence to it. When you are trying to beat time you will be looking for quick results and will favour those who have your urgency, valuing the staff member who aims to get through work within a time frame rather than the one who goes deeper to determine a better procedure to follow. You will prefer to have meetings with someone who sticks to time rather than someone who wants to achieve something out of the discussion and goes on and on and on therefore wasting time for everybody.

Although viewing time as the enemy does create a challenge to stir your spirit, it will eventually be damaging.

The immediate negative consequences are that your mind is in a constant state of conflict and you cannot fully appreciate your experiences, your relationships and your achievements. This is because you are always dwelling on how you are going to win against the clock; your satisfactions are short-lived because you are looking to the next time-pressured chore. Your life becomes one long series of chores.

Time as a mystery

By contrast, ignoring the time factor or the restrictions caused by time can land you in a muddle.

When you are totally involved in what you are doing, you are detached from your surroundings and concentrating on the job in hand in a totally single-minded way and so are unaware of time. As a manager, you are letting one task supersede everything else and the crisis management needed to correct the situation will waste even more time.

When you treat time as a mystery and do not estimate or forecast what can be achieved at any stage, time comes and goes, targets are not set or met and you are not leading anyone anywhere. This attitude can be prevalent amongst even the most rational people during periods of sudden, intense and wide-spread change when many fixed points in the day week or month change suddenly.

When you refuse to make appointments or keep to the agreed time you upset others. Allow it to become a habit and you will be regarded as unreliable. You see everything as unpredictable and beyond control, and therefore not your fault, eg, you were late because the train was late. You are in serious danger of gaining a reputation which you cannot afford to have and will find difficult to get rid of.

Time is finite, and you must come to terms with the rules of using it to your advantage. Unless you recognize the scarcity of time, you will wrongly prioritize your tasks and achieve little, however hard you believe you are working.

Time as your command

When you view time as your slave, your central concern becomes control, but time is elusive so be prepared for not gaining the total control you imagine you want. You will end up living in the future. By planning each day and each activity you may become preoccupied with the planning rather than with the activity, eg, during meetings, instead of listening, you will be thinking ahead when it is necessary to act spontaneously.

You are in danger of needing visible proof of the good use of your time and feeling satisfied only when you can say, 'I didn't stop working for one minute today!' All this adds up to the likelihood that you will be exhausted by trying to use every minute, and you will also be in danger of becoming a chronic workaholic because you will soon find it impossible to relax after work or on vacation. This attitude often wins praise in the West, being perceived as a high level of industriousness and achievement. It is accepted that it is good to use time efficiently and bad to waste it in ways that are not *visibly* productive.

The drawbacks to this belief that you can enslave time are beginning to evidence themselves. More people are stopping to question the admiration of activity for activity's sake. It is also beginning to be noticed that there are other values and achievements to be reckoned with as well as the purely visible. So you are not automatically maximizing the use of your time when you are being busy, busy, busy.

Time as your judge

When you check with the clock about when you should work, when you should eat, when you can have a drink, when you can go for a walk, etc, then you are allowing time to rule your responses. Time becomes your referee. You are trying to synchronize your actions with the time signals. Whenever you are unable to react 'correctly', you will start to cheat and cover up to yourself, eg, 'I'm just sneaking a break'. This is a false sense of bravado and a dubious focus for your energies. It can result in a complete slump in your energies after completing a highly-concentrated task. You must learn to play as well as work.

Time exists as a restricting and disciplining mechanism, and the flow of personal time is important for you. However, if you can overcome a concern with specific hours and minutes, you will be better able to recognize your time as a whole. Then you can take full responsibility for your time and do what you really want with it.

Procrastination

Are you a procrastinator? You will recognize the habit of playing games with the clock and trying to outsmart it – eg, I'll just do this and then I will tackle that report' – you are always hoping that there is more time available than there really is.

You can train yourself to become less vulnerable to the habit of putting things off by taking the following tips:

- Be realistic about the length of time it is actually going to take to complete a task, eg, writing a report in half an hour, finding a house in a week, or completing an assignment in one month are probably all unrealistic.
- Prepare predictions of how long things will take based on experience and available facts. You may even experience or measure the individual items which make the whole, eg, how long does it take you to reach the client's office; are they punctual in starting meetings, do they stick to the agenda, is the chairperson quick to wind up? All are indicators of how long a meeting will last.
- Use small 'holes' of time between big commitments to do part of a large task rather than waiting for a commensurate large amount of time to be magically available. This 'Swiss cheese' technique gives value to any amount of time, however small. You will not be taken unawares when you have time between appointments, etc, and will get into the habit of using it profitably. Similarly, you will find better use for the time when you have cancelled an appointment, or are waiting for someone to answer the telephone.

- Set time limits – a deadline for doing something reduces your choices. Doing this prevents you from using work to punish yourself by keeping a horrible job waiting to be done eventually. Punishment is not a good motivation.
- We have all experienced Murphy's Law – when anything that can go wrong, does go wrong. When you put things off, you are in danger of being ruled by Murphy. Leaving things to the last minute is dangerous, as that last minute can always be eroded by something else. When you overcome your resistance to getting started you will find it easier to get going and to get co-operation from others.
- Delegating is another way to combat procrastination. This means you have to identify which tasks you don't want to do and whom to give them to. They might even be better than you at doing them. When you are in pursuit of perfection you can make the mistake that you are the only person who should undertake a job – and fall into the trap of overloading yourself. Do not be afraid that you will have too much time on your hands if you reduce the pressure of urgent demands by handing down responsibility. You are doing many things at once – getting the task dealt with and developing the person are two aspects.
- Identify your prime times for doing certain things, however basic. Acknowledge that there are times of the day when you can do more than at other times, and plan accordingly.
- Enjoy your free time. When you deprive yourself of true relaxation, you will run out of energy and begin to procrastinate – you will then have to 'steal' your leisure time. This is a spiralling process – so stop now.

When you are procrastinating you are not working well and are not able to relax fully either. In order to have real fun, get jobs done and then switch off. Light relief is an important aspect of life. Get into the habit of enjoying events, places, etc. It really is true that all work and no play makes us dull, dreary and desperate.

Whether you have to produce the company's annual report, complete your novel or bake a birthday cake, the risk is that the responsibility of the project will loom so large, and the details appear so complicated, that you will begin to wonder whether you will actually get through it. You may even worry whether your career will survive what seems to be a crucial test of your ability. As your fears mount the project suffers. So how do you turn the impossible into the possible?

1. Take the mystery out of it. Divide the project into sections of smaller pieces until you can visualize a step-by-step method of completing it. These easily completed components can be tackled as small sub-projects which are less intimidating. You can easily identify which parts to delegate.

2. Use the Swiss Cheese method. This allows you to start a project by completing some of the more enjoyable parts first. As you accomplish the parts one by one, you will gain a sense of momentum and enthusiasm. This will enable you to tackle the parts that once seemed less fun or even beyond your abilities.

3. Build in extra time. Setting deadlines for yourself is one thing, but it is useful to set them ahead of the real time required when you are delegating tasks.

4. Set up half-hour goals when your creativity is running low. Say to yourself you will stop in half an hour, then see how much more you can actually do.

5. Keep track of the project's overall progress, using a personal computer, critical path analysis, or a large simple wall-chart.

Priorities

Anything or anybody who distracts you from achieving your objectives is a timewaster. Sometimes you will go looking for these distractions but most of the time you will be trying to avoid them. So what, and who, are the most easily-identified timewasters? In *The Time Trap*, Dr Alec Mackenzie sites the top timewasters as follows:

1. Telephone interruptions
2. Paperwork/red tape/reading
3. Crisis management

4. Drop-in visitors
5. Attempting too much
6. Under-staffing
7. Lacking objectives/priorities/plans
8. Visual distractions/noise
9. Lacking necessary facts
10. People unavailable for discussions
11. Procrastination/indecision
12. Inability to say 'no'
13. Meetings
14. Personal disorganization/cluttered desk
15. Untrained/inadequate staff
16. Lack of/unclear communications
17. Incomplete/delayed information
18. Leaving tasks unfinished
19. Poor filing system
20. Ineffective delegation

Learn to distinguish the urgent from the important. Urgent matters demand immediate action and have an air of legitimacy, whereas important matters can be postponed – it seems. Do not confuse them.

Above all, remember the old banker's maxim: 'Yesterday's time is a cancelled cheque. Tomorrow's time is a promissory note. Today's time is ready cash' – use it.

6.3 SURVIVAL STRATEGY

Contribution to 'the bottom line'

In a senior management position the complexity of taking charge and doing what is best for the business is, progressively, the key to your own effectiveness and requires a certain amount of toughness.

Headhunters note your management style, measurable contribution and success, as well as your precise involvement in the outcome. Your company, Board, shareholders and staff will be affected by the way your input to 'the bottom line' is evidenced in the balance sheet and in the development of the organization.

Ralph Halpern, the Burton Group's well-paid entrepreneurial retail boss, agrees with Professor Charles Handy of the London Business School that managing change is by far the most important skill anyone running a company can possess. However, his main concern is the share of the profits and dividends which he can announce at his Annual General Meeting. He concludes that your skills are of little value if they are not reflected in the positive results and profits of your company in some way.

Accountability becomes real when you take on a job with extra 'clout', giving you sole responsibility for the outcome of the activity at the end of the period. It is one thing not to achieve your targets, another not to receive a bonus, but it is really serious when there is a reduction in the regard for your reputation as a successful executive, which will occur when your accountability/ results are weak.

Therefore, agree targets, access to markets, etc, in the knowledge of what you *cannot* do as much as what you *can* do. Prevent a disastrous hiccup in your career by realistic evaluation and negotiation at all stages of projects or developments, and be sure you are in a strong enough position to make adjustments when necessary at crucial stages on the way. Pressure to be always outstanding can be irresistible – knowing how you contribute best to the bottom line is your remedy.

Discovering what the bottom line is, then, is important. This may be the easy part of your exploration into company requirements as you may discover that what is expected of you is frightening, unpleasant, demanding or even unacceptable. The hard and difficult part of management is when your abilities, experience and knowledge are stretched. The unacceptable is when it goes against your value systems to take such action. The decisions or stands you may have to take to avoid the possibility of jeopardizing your career cannot be delegated. You can weigh up your chances with trusted mentors, colleagues and partners, but ultimately, the decisions are yours alone. There will be situations you will dread – but the relief after completion is marvellous.

Taking the welfare of your employees into the calculations when judging the competitiveness or commercial ramifications of

the organization is often the area in which you will be acknow-
ledging your obligations within the corporate structure. From
time to time you will suffer to win.

The whole debate on equal opportunities in the workplace
facilitating women, ethnic minorities and the disabled within the
main-frame of employment has given rise to much soul-searching
in management during the last decade. The bottom line necessity
for having these focii within the payroll is now surfacing. It is
recognized that it is becoming cost-effective to include women
returners and anyone capable of being trained into the job,
regardless of background.

*Making business work is short-term: living with the outcome is long-
term. Finding out your levels of capability and tolerance will better
prepare you for your extension to your limits or when matching your full
potential within the corporate culture. Then you will be maximizing your
contribution to the bottom line – your value to the organization.*

Knowing the rules

You have to be more than good at your job to survive the climb
up each rung of the ladder and to stay at the top when you get
there. Most executives believe that working hard and 'being on
the ball' will ensure their success. However, in order that you
continue to be propelled upwards you must seek out what is
required to fit in with the chemistry of the firm.

Knowing the rules is a good way of understanding the climate
you are in, for gaining insight into what is required from you in
order to be efficient in your role and to be seen to be effective in
your overall executive position. You need to adjust your actions
and attitudes to fit your surroundings, in order to maintain your
acceptance within the group. This presupposes that you know
how – that you have found out what is expected. You must
become familiar with systems – everything from mechanical
behaviour to the use of information technology, as well as
knowing what those to whom you report will expect, appreciate,
respect and reward. How do you achieve these?

There are two recognized ways:

1. To observe all the time and note the key aspects of what is

happening around you.
2. At the same time solicit feedback and general information on your own performance and on company forecasts.

Another way of knowing the game and so increasing your influence is sometimes possible – that is, by keeping in very close contact with other senior executives and finding out about their achievements and attributes.

The way up continues as you visualize yourself on the next rung – and the next, and the next.

In your functional mode, eg, marketing, finance, technical advice, etc, you can shape up your own development against those in similar categories. The gossip really is at least as important as what appears in final reports. How you measure your executive success is by results and sphere of influence.

It is the intangibles in your professional life rather than the listings in your CV which actually matter.

Awareness

Your personal rule must be that your career is entirely up to you. You will have read how to shape your future by setting goals and planning your route on a conscious plane. From the age of 30 you will be on the path to the top which you have already identified. You will be keeping your visibility high, side-stepping blockages, and will be achieving steady promotion with or without the use of mobility.

The main way to move up within the company is by managing people well, finding the best outlet for your energy and constantly meeting the expectations of your seniors. This will happen mostly through your responsibility for profit and loss and your delivery to the bottom line requirement. In the public sector, the earlier you have to make and meet budget requirements the better – even though final accountability does remain at the top.

It is equally important to have awareness of the need for true management and to grab an opportunity as soon as possible. When you move out of staff jobs, you know you are on your way and getting into the mainstream of the business. This can be even more important than an increase in salary. It is certainly what the headhunter looks for as the first step towards boardroom expertise.

Based on the assumptions that you are keeping your qualifications up to date (eg, getting sponsored by your firm to do an MBA) and keeping in touch with your professional associations, then you are not going to be caught short if you are offered a career move unexpectedly. Awareness is the external part of being prepared and gives you the caché of not only being available but ready to perform. But there is no short cut to the top, however − it is hard work, making choices, hard work, building on experience, balancing work and home, hard work, stamina, hard work, courage, hard work: then achievement and fun are there for you at each turning.

Take command of your career. You may have to change company or sector or speciality or location in order to increase your chances of furthering your career. Your awareness of the value of the risk and opportunity will prove your judgement. You may have pushed your way up, moved sideways, taken a sabbatical and done just what was necessary to win the reputation for being a successful executive on your way to be among the best. Now you have to watch out that neither are you 'gazumped' nor do you become static or complacent.

Confidence tricks

It is lonely at the top. Who do you confide in now? Confidence is your most needed commodity. Top people exude an air of confidence − successful entrepreneurs and company bosses do have this attribute in common. They know this and work on their image to lessen their chances of being seen as vulnerable. Like bees to the honeypot, others find this image very attractive and cluster around so that they will be identified as successful because of their close proximity to success − 'nothing succeeds like success'. From Alan Bond to the Rockefellers to Margaret Thatcher to Richard Branson to Armand Hammer − their success is rated by the scale of their following at any one time. Paul Getty and Howard Hughes went to extreme lengths to escape the attentions of their sycophants.

Self-confidence does enable you to take risks. You can deal better with the unfamiliar, giving more effective leadership and hold on to calmness during a crisis when you have faith in yourself. Your willingness to listen to others and to accept their perceptions of either the problem being solved or of yourself will be evidenced in your being able to admit mistakes and to agree that you are not infallible.

When direct experience plus success produces confidence, then risk-taking will increase it.

When you take on and carry through a difficult assignment, you increase your wherewithal to meet challenge. Notice will be taken of the number of times you are prepared to undertake risky new projects or areas of responsibilities and your performance. You are fortunate when you have a boss who encourages you, even when you are unwilling to go ahead and take the chance. This is the best way of increasing your reputation – gaining the opportunity to shine by someone else believing in you.

When you delegate or rely on others to get the job done, sharing the recognition on completion, as well as obtaining the good assignments in the first place, you are well on your way to being a first-class manager. You have to be able to inter-relate up and down the line if you are to survive within the corporate economy, so use your confidence to do so.

Help from above has often been indicated as an essential aid to reaching the senior ranks. No matter how high you climb, there will always be others with more power, spending ability or whatever. Learning from them will be useful to you and the knowledge, when digested, needs to be channelled on down the line, so make sure you keep it flowing freely.

It is hard, complicated and crucial that you succeed with people, have confidence in yourself and continue to be aware at all stages in your development.

Integrity

It is easier to hold on to a set of values and conditions which you recognize, and which are undemanding of your commitment and effort, than to do otherwise. Your dissatisfaction will grow when you feel threatened by the performance of others whose you see as superior to your own – similarly, with your company, concept or country.

Therefore, you need clarity and openness in your thinking – and management style – to prevent this from growing. John Harvey-Jones believed in open knowledge when he headed up ICI – each person there had access to the knowledge of the state of the company, good or bad, at any time. He believed in the 'need to know' principle. So the more you explain the more you need to know to pass on – the more open the business culture the more you can influence others to win. The reality is that closed or static thinking is the most comfortable for the immediate future but the highest risk strategy is the most likely to be productive in the future.

So review your ability to be open, demonstrate your integrity and keep your values up to the minute.

Vision

A McKinsey guru, Quince Hunsicker, highlights the need for vision in senior management and describes it as 'the ability of top managers to construct and evaluate the implications for the enterprise of the scenarios of the future'. He states that your vision is enhanced by:

- Seeing and understanding the pattern of forces underlying superficially unrelated events and phenomena
- Knowing when to assess or challenge assumptions that may have been part of the tradition of a company or industry for so long that they have been accepted as gospel
- Recognizing 'hybrid' behaviour and avoiding falling prey to the tyranny of averages in observing and dealing with it
- Balancing qualitative and quantitative judgements in reaching conclusions, eg, analysis *versus* intuition

You will have to aim consciously to encompass these aspects into your vision of your future.

Field-Marshall Montgomery of Alamein (whose son David is a

non-executive director of Korn/Ferry International) believed in 'lifting their hearts and hardening their wills' when motivating his forces. Have you worked out which order of precedence is more effective within your style of thinking? An important consideration when contemplating your vision for your career, or mission statement for your firm, is contained in this emphasis.

The problems of diagnosis are simple compared with the problems of actually making things happen. All too often you will get only one kick at the ball and so you will have to learn on the move – so the clearer your vision the easier it will be for you to kick the ball into goal. The learning experience never ends – knowing where to fit each item learnt into the overall picture is the way to complete it.

The nearer the top you climb, the greater the opportunity to be ineffective and uncensured – so you must have a strong sense of your own values and how to make things happen through your leadership so that your vision for the organization will be realized.

6.4 KEEPING ON TRACK

Checking direction

The one enduring feature of any corporation or enterprise is the people and their skills. However, you need to be continually checking that you and your teams are constantly regenerating and keeping your skills up to date. Individuals need stimulation in order to continue to contribute to the project or work in hand, and you need to renew your leadership thinking.

Much individual and commercial change is brought on by actions of others outside your control – the key to success is for you to be heading the pace for change rather than letting it happen.

Increasingly, companies intending to expand and progress will be aiming to meet the needs of the people within them. W H Smith and British Steel are two organizations that have already had positive results in their balance sheets owing to this type of corporate thinking. Payment is important, but it is the inner needs of the individual (which you may not even know yourself) which keep your interest in your career and in doing your job well. Enhancing your capabilities and expectations is what you should be considering when checking the direction in which you are heading.

The effect of the growth of technology – including domestic machines – is to provide a range of choices and opportunities unheard of even several decades ago. Therefore, as John Harvey-Jones says in *Making it Happen*: 'Industry and technology are the enablers. They enable us to have choices, but ultimately the choices, for good or bad, have to be made by us'.

This adaptation towards our needs as individuals will release your energies, creativity and imagination. Commercial success does depend on attracting the very best people, like yourself, and motivating you, so it is essential for the company to use the selection methods to find you and then nurture you and enable you to develop on their behalf because you are satisfying yourself. As there are now more women at senior level than in the past, so industry and commerce will benefit from their focus on this nurturing, mature aspect of their management skills.

There is a paradox seen in the more secure future forecast for the small niche business and the huge conglomerate, rather than the middle-sized, steadily-expanding company, in that your needs will be met in the very small-scale and the very large-resourced ventures, because at both these levels you can have choice, freedom and the ability to use your self-determination. Otherwise, in the middle you are tied to the objectives of the growing company above all else.

Now check your direction again and make sure you are on course. Are you relating your own needs to the competitive imperatives of the business in which you are an influence? Management is about people, and business success depends on harnessing, motivating and leading them.

Glass ceiling

Large interview sessions with executives in the upper echelons of American companies in the late 1980s have indicated that there is a glass ceiling – a transparent barrier which apparently keeps some executives, especially women, from rising above a certain level in corporations. This is not simply a hurdle or wall stopping an individual going further due to the lack of ability to handle a higher level job. It applies, in particular, to the group within those companies who are kept from advancing higher because they do not fit the male, Caucasian stereotype. It usually falls just below the level of general manager.

This is the stage at which the executive is expected to deal with the development, manufacture, sales and marketing of a product with all the internal management necessary. Other general managers will be co-ordinating more than one product, maybe business strategy for many, many products. The point is that the general management position represents a major and difficult transition in responsibility from purely functional to general overall control and accountability. This is the level which represents less than 1 per cent of the workforce.

This is where you have been aiming to arrive for some time. Are you prepared?

Yes, it is difficult from what you can observe from the outside and from below to believe that you could ever be part of that influential senior board – but an increasing number of people, including women and ethnic minorities, are getting there and being effective. There will always be some people who get close enough to see the politicking, the power gymnastics and the sheer hard work, and perhaps loneliness – and decide it is not for them, so they sheer off and do something else. Often they decide that they want their own tiny firm over which they have full control. This has been a successful female strategy for some time. Nevertheless, this inner sanctum of senior management does exist and is made up of the core of business leaders who wield the greatest power, so assume you will join them.

General management is also the point at which managers are admitted into this 'club' of many companies. Prospective members are reviewed by the current members to make sure that their faces will fit. This intangible exercise has gone on since the year dot. However, the power of the headhunter is creeping in and changing things.

Now that senior general managers are known to be the key to company results, the Board will invite the headhunters to find outsiders or to measure the quality of the insider in a mixed field. This is having the effect of creating a glass ceiling for many people, because it is more analytical rather than just an instructive way to the top. This is helping women and other specialists to be considered for general management and allowed such experience earlier than has formerly been the case. The next step will be to be members of the Board.

You do have to be considered smart, be known to have worked hard and had visible achievements, be capable and well-motivated, if you are going to continue to 'the top'. There are three extras which top general managers possess:

1. *Credibility* – by having had the opportunity to work alongside senior directors either in or out of company time.
2. *Sponsorship* – when they have been put forward by senior people on the basis of their knowledge of the work done and the fact that they have used their influence on the junior's behalf.
3. *Plain good fortune* – being in the right place at the right time.

Acceptable behaviour is that which is common to all, regardless of gender:

a) Taking risks but being constantly outstanding as an executive. Risk is the name of the game at the top. Sometimes you may have responsibility for large sums of money or the livelihood of many depend on your actions. The earlier you practise taking risks the better prepared you will be.

This covers many things – from job changes to listening to the headhunter and knowing when to move on to undertaking assignments which are quite different one from the other, eg, from academic to industrial content. Highfliers are expected to be risk-takers. Any candidate for a senior job has to be good – women even better than the men and even better than the stereotype of the woman.

b) Being tough – which is the ability to make difficult decisions and not just being macho for the sake of it. You have to be strong-willed, undertake the results of your decisions and be steady under pressure, rather than proving to be an 'unguided missile' in a crisis.

c) Being ambitious – without expecting the career path to be easy or necessarily fair.

d) Taking responsibility – and taking the advice of others. On occasions you must be seen to be following the thinking of others. Your judgement can be called into question from time to time – then you need to acquire 'the wisdom of Solomon'.

Only you can make the most of your career. This book was commissioned and written to help you meet your needs through planning to meet your goals by knowing about and applying serious management commonsense. I have tried to use plain language and collate current thinking in logical progression. Many situations and processes may be familiar to you already – all are possible for you to win further recognition and so increase your visibility.

It is important that companies and organizations have some insight into how headhunting works – and how we regard the individual route to the best jobs and eventually to the boardroom or the relevant top positions. I see general selection methods, eg, recruiting/advertising, as the shotgun approach, whereas in executive search the headhunters use the laser beam method to fix on the exact people to meet the criteria.

You will have realized that your hard work, plus recognition, equals wider opportunities for you to progress. Then you have to take the risk when faced with choices. Firms seeking good senior people must not be persuaded by perceived stereotypes and also take risks when building senior teams. We are all different from how you imagine us, anyway. So let the headhunters widen the trawl to introduce you to everyone possible who will meet your corporate requirements, and not just the more familiar, obvious role-players or self-identified applicants.

Equally, women *must not* be afraid of earning well and must learn to visualize themselves in those top jobs. You can do it – probably are already, although your door/desk has a different label.

It is forecast that the shortage of labour in the 1990s onwards will mean that 55 per cent of the workforce will be women at managerial and professional levels, which will be a big change from the present preponderance of women in clerical, cleaning and other low-paid or part-time work.

The Government, through Norman Fowler and now Michael Howard at the Department of Employment, has been spending £3 billion per year on employer-led training programmes and on encouraging skills-based education and packages. They want to 'have the high skill, high productivity, high-wage economy Britain needs to forge ahead into the Twenty-first Century'.

The whole dilemma of using all available people within industry covers the training of school leavers, women returners and those who are post-50 and have been categorized as 'old'.

There are moves afoot to help women returners. Ann Watts, Director of Equal Opportunities, Midland Bank, was the pioneer in providing crèches for the children. She had been involved previously, at National Westminster Bank, with the construction of career break packages also.

Lesley Abdela, M.B.E., has worked hard to advance women in work and in politics, and Joanna Foster – current Chairperson of the Equal Opportunities Commission – both agree – that the 1990s will see the demographic time-bomb changing the use of people within the workplace and their sphere of influence.

Valerie Amos, Chief Executive of the EDC, is further concerned by the short-term effects for all the minorities in any situation. She wants to see senior managers like you giving a permanent lead to finding the best for each job at each stage within your organization regardless of such considerations.

6.5 BEING THE BEST

Strategic management is the process of translating a vision of an organization's future into a living reality. Being seen as a successful part of that process identifies you as being a business leader in an uncertain and stormy business world. You will have proved your courage and stamina.

The rate of change globally is accelerating. You would not have been able to predict the opening of the Eastern European Markets or the disruptions in the Middle East in 1990. Yet you do have to forecast and take a view of the situation ahead in order to plan production, manage the company and be prepared to undertake the work to match the economic environment round the next corner.

Your assessment of future trends will affect the outcome of your decisions. Managing within this uncertain framework really does require 'the best' people at the top to have the insight and to give the leadership if the organization is to win through.

Philip Sadler, Vice President of Ashridge Management College, sets six descriptions of situations in which you may find yourself:

1. *FOG* – when it just is not possible to see the way ahead – eg an impending election which freezes policies and actions until the results are known.
2. *TERRA INCOGNITA* – when you are faced by an entirely novel scenario – eg the implications of the integration of the UK into the EEC after 1992.
3. *RAPIDS* – very fast frequent changes within important parameters over which you do not have control – eg peaks and troughs in commodity prices.
4. *OSCILLATION* – a similar set of upheavals but you will have the assumption that there is an underlying norm or element of stability around which there are large variations – eg the business cycle.
5. *AMBIGUITY* – you have real and immediate troubles to deal with when previously reliable indicators prove to be so no longer – eg the blue book of UK economic trends including those related to industrial production has been queried recently with regard to its usefulness in measuring movement into or recovery from recession.
6. *FUZZINESS* – the uncertainty which comes with incomplete data. You do have to face an increasing number of decisions which you will take based on inadequate information (even though information technology has advanced). This is because of the needs and aspirations of customers and competitors in an accelerating business world.

The way you react to uncertainty is either rational or irrational. This does not mean that you are always rational or irrational – it can fluctuate according to the moment. I think that management through these uncertain phases is most difficult and does show up the best people. When you accept that there will always be uncertainty to a greater or lesser extent – and set about reducing it, you are being rational. When you try to find the certain elements within the situation, or even try to opt out of the whole responsibility – then you are being irrational.

A good survivor therefore will exploit the uncertainty using creativity with your own organization intending to push the uncertainty towards your competitors – eg the Coca Cola/Pepsi world marketing patterns.

Being the best is a stressful, highlighted pedestal you will be standing on when you reach the upper echelons, so recognize that you should provide opportunities for yourself to control the situation and release the stress – 40 million working days are lost in British industry each year due to stress related problems. There is proof that cutting the working week has cut the risk of coronary disease. You will have met doctors and dentists, the professionals with the highest suicide rate, who have tried alcohol or other drug-related aids to help reduce stress.

So how will you avoid the peptic ulcers, the high blood pressure or whatever your highly demanding visible career is likely to produce in your body? You will only be good, better or best with those at the top if you are alive and well to stand the course. Donald Norfolk, in *Executive Stress*, concludes that:

'When executives [you] perform under conditions of optimum arousal produced by the healthy stimulus of excitement, reward, challenge or change, they [you] show an improvement in performance. But when stress . . . is prolonged . . . performance declines.'

Your individual contribution and the environment within which you work affect your levels of stress – so what can you do to further maintain your place? Stay cool; space your effort; work hard and play hard; laugh – watch *Cheers*!

The earlier you have an understanding of the complexity of the use and limitations of power and authority when you are in a senior management role the better. How do you keep your route to the top clear of destruction by bosses with whom you have dealings on the way.

Professor Thomas Kempner, Henley Management College and Brunel University has given some thought to the survival of subordinates and has come up with a ten point briefing:

1. Don't give your boss nasty shocks.
2. Talk to the boss about your concerns before they become catastrophies.
3. Don't expect instant decisions for items on which you should have reported in detail earlier.
4. Prove that you know your position within the corporate thinking – and not just your own perspective.
5. Show a balanced sample of memos and letters relating to your work to the boss – not just the good.
6. Prepare well for meetings: have alternative actions plans – do not push your pet schemes only.
7. Issues needing discussion and decision require you to provide facts, figures, etc well in advance.
8. Be professional – having pressed your views hard and others ideas have been accepted, then you carry those out as if they were your own.
9. Positive thinking, providing solutions to problems wins you friends: whining and complaining about difficulties does not.
10. Please be brief and to the point. The more important bosses are the more precious they see the use of their time.

For centuries, the unwritten practice was that you gained job security in return for loyalty to the firm just like the aristocrats have protected their servants.

In the 1990s we are seeing, already, the effects of global market forces, international influences and national movements as well as corporate policies.

As I have been saying over and over again, your career really is under your own control and needs masterminding by you. Now opportunities are created, rewards and challenges are available, you have to take them but also arrange your own security and pension. Organizations are facilitating the individual more and more by providing the tools which will enable you to take advantage of training, performance-related rewards and so on.

When the firm is new – your knowledge, control of information and your skills provide you with a power base. This you have to keep reinforcing as new knowledge and skills are appearing all the time. In the company with a flat management structure, you do not have rungs of the hierarchical ladder to climb but you extend your knowledge sideways informally through your colleagues – training is a more formal method. In your career plan you regard new corporate structures as learning places – starting with small and growing to the big. There is no short cut anymore to a lifetime career package within a group – more like the party game of pass the parcel where the package moves round, is exposed layer by layer until the golden nugget at the centre is revealed for all to acknowledge.

The reward system is no longer just money in return for hours worked. You will be negotiating more and more as the scale of your operation grows. Just over 50 per cent of executive packages consist of cash, pension, performance related elements, stock options, etc, which is much less like a pay packet/salary cheque than a division of company profits. However, there is still no guarantee of long-term stability of your relationship with your employer. You can regard the greater compensation/pay scales at present as another career tool which can buy you options and freedom on your own time scale. Financial and career planning interact.

Visibility is now sometimes included in senior post job descriptions – as a serious attraction. Just as some people do get blocked in their career due to low visibility causing even their excellent performance to go unnoticed – a job which gives you the visibility which marks you out is good news.

The product, the brand name, the level of publicity involved in your job will give you a comparable amount of credibility and exposure. Headhunters are used by clients to find the best for the post – so the bigger and better the client the bigger and better the possibilities for you. By staging the position in which you can be found and by being clearly visible, the headhunter will be able to bring you into the frame more quickly. You add value at each level, contribute to the bottom line, manage your people and meetings well and your reputation will have added value too. The more your face is recognized in a crowd the more your calls from the headhunter will come.

You will grow your career, not from being employed alone, but by being employable and for having the reputation for achievement – for your organization as well as yourself.

'The renown of the great should always be measured by the means which they have used to acquire it.' La Roche Foucauld.

Index